ARMENIAN VILLAGE LIFE BEFORE 1914

ARMENIAN VILLAGE LIFE BEFORE 1914

by Susie Hoogasian Villa
and Mary Kilbourne Matossian

Wayne State University Press   Detroit, 1982

Library of Congress Cataloging in Publication Data

Villa, Susie Hoogasian.
  Armenian village life before 1914.

  Bibliography: p.
  Includes index.
  1. Armenia—Social life and customs.   I. Matossian,
Mary Allerton Kilbourne.   II. Title.
DS171.V54   1982   956.6'2   82-8521
ISBN 0-8143-1700-6   AACR2

Grateful acknowledgment is made to the John M. Dorsey
Publishing Fund for assistance in the publication of this volume.

Special acknowledgment is made to Mrs. Agnes Nigoghosian who
made available the periodical *Keghouni* (1901–1909) from which
the photographs were taken.

Special acknowledgment is made to Mr. and Mrs. Israel Nigosian
for assistance in preparation of the glossary and the map, and for
typesetting the Armenian alphabet.

CONTENTS

CONTRIBUTORS TO THE SUSIE HOOGASIAN VILLA FUND FOR ARMENIAN CULTURE AND FOLKLORE

Robert and Hrach Ajemian
Walter and Martha Akkashian
Agop and Diana Alexanian
Guy and Elizabeth Amboian
George and Zabel Arakelian
Arous Ardash
Armenian American Veterans
  Memorial Association
Armenian Renaissance
  Association, Sophia Chapter
Harold and Marion Artinian
Rose Aznavoorian
Armenouhi Babigian
Maxim Bahadurian
James and Irene Baharozian
Grace Bayleran
Rebecca Bayleran
Jirayre and Mannik Bedikian
Snar and Siroun Bedikian
Ralph and Jean Beland
Gary and Zabel Belian
Ara and Virginia Berberian
Harry Berberian
Peter and Ann Betrus
Russell and Viola Bine
Joseph and Jeanne Bryk

Joseph T. Bryk
Lawrence and Nancy Bryk
Mary Bryk
Louis Calfin
George and Mae Creech
Hranoush Dabanian
Hamazasp and Vrejouhi Darian
Marion Davis
Thomas and Virgine Denha
Detroit Armenian Women's
  Club
Harry and Ann Dombalagian
Charles and Martha Donaldson
Mike and Ann Donoian
Steve and Karen Douse
Henry Dudek
George and Marian Elian
Reggie S. Essayan
Arthur Filjanian
Petemitza Filjanian
Ford Service and Parts Division
General Electric Company
Mike Geragosian
Nancy Geragosian
Ara and Verkin Gholdoian
Masis and Alberta Godoshian

Ida Gononian
Archie and Susan Gopigian
Yeranouhi Haidostian Gotting
Robert Guenther and Family
Werner and Beatrice Guenther
John and Clementine Gutowski
Berj and Alice Haidostian
Howard and Elva Hale
C. Arthur Hietala
David and Joan Hill
Homestyle Foods
Cindy Hoogasian
Hripsima Hoogasian
Martin Hoogasian
Vaughn and Lorene Hoogasian
Richard and Sirapy Hough
Krikor and Hasmig Imirzian
Dean and Rose Janigian
Alex and Lily Jemal
George and Lucine Juskalian
Susan Kachigian
George and Alice Kadian
Marderus and Gloria Kadian
Armen Kasabach
Abraham and Zabel Kalajian
Diran and Ardemis Kalousdian
John and Rebecca Kapolka
Ashen Kavafian
Vincent and Rose Kaye
Suzan Kazanjian
Hagop and Agnes Kemsuzian
Zabel Kouzian
Arshalous Krimian
Jean Kubik
Paul and Esther Kulhanjian
Paul and Simone Lada
Meyer and Leatrice Levy

Zaven and Helen Lucas
Leonor McAlpine
Tom and Ginger McLaughlin
Grace McPherson
H. P. Mahanes
Richard and Rose Maloian
Charles and Helen Master
Garbis and Armen Mechigian
Edmond and Axelle Megerian
Krikor and Nennette
   Merametdjian
Michael and Emma Minasian
Herman and Hilda Misirliyan
Cross and Shakay Mooradian
Marti Mooradian
Richard and Audrey
   Mooradian
George and Mary Mugerian
Andrew Murray
Mary Murray
Michael and Nina Murray
Elizabeth Najarian
Paul and Haigouhi Nazarian
Andrew and Kathleen
   Nersesian
John and Myrna Nersesian
Alice Nigoghosian
Israel and Hermine Nigosian
Mamigon and Satenig Ossian
Hortense M. O'Shea
Satenik H. Ourian
Robert N. Paklaian
Sarah Paklaian
Dickranouhi Papelian
Vahe and Anoush Papelian
Janet Parker
Harriet Pawlowska

Jeannette Pawlowski
Layne Peterson
Peterson & Vaughan, Inc.
Jeff and Pat Petrash
William and Alice Radak
Sydney and Priscilla Radlow
Louis and Ann Rakay
Donna Rakay
Bernard and Margaret Reilly
Robert Rennie
Siroun and Ayda Sarafian
Nevart R. Sarkesian
Tom and Zepur Sarkesian
George and Zabel Sarkisian
Robert and Lucine Sarkisian
Joanna Savage
Vahe and Varsenik Sekdorian
Hike and Mida Semerjian
Mary Sharoian
Jack and Zarrouhe
  Shoushanian
Rose (Nemeth) Sidun
Karl and Emma Sogoian

Mary Surabian
Krikor and Sona Terterian
Armen and Norma Topouzian
Richard and Caroline Torley
Jesse and Mary Trevino
Alice G. Tucker
Armenouhi Varbedian
Anahid Vart
Alice Vartanian
Ross and Margaret Vartian
Frank and Inez Veraldi
Adolph and Katherine Villa
James D. Villa
John J. Villa
John K. Villa
Robert and Ellen Villa
Sam and Diana Villa
Sammy Villa
Wayne B. Wheeler, Jr.
Harriet Wojtowicz
Anna Wrobel
Aram and Sara Yavruyan
Ara and Peruz Zerounian

PREFACE

Susie Hoogasian Villa was born Soseh (Susie) Hoogasian in Detroit, Michigan, on December 22, 1921, the daughter of Kazar Hoogasian of Akor, a village near Kharpert, and Hripsima Nakushian Demerjian Hoogasian, a native of the town of Kharpert. Her parents and maternal grandmother were refugees from the Turkish massacre of the Armenian people during World War I. Both of her parents had been married before, and both had lost a spouse and family during those painful days. After immigrating separately to America, they met, married, and made their home in the Delray section of Detroit. Armenian was widely spoken there, and Armenian language classes were held after regular school hours. Susie and her brother, Vaughn, attended the Zavarian Armenian School, from which she graduated.

While she was growing up, Susie Hoogasian became intrigued with the stories told by her family and friends as they gathered in the evenings to visit and talk about the Armenia they remembered. Encouraged by Evelyn E. Gardner of the Wayne State University Department of English, she began to collect stories from the Armenians of Delray, and she continued to do so while attending the university, where she earned a B.S. in education (1944) and an M.A. in English (1948). In the summer of 1946, she was awarded a graduate fellowship to the Indiana University Folklore Institute, where she studied under Stith Thompson.

In late 1946, Susie Hoogasian married John J. Villa. They had three children: John K., born in 1948; Nancy, born in 1956; and James, born in 1962. Shortly after James's birth, Mrs. Villa began the arduous task of gathering necessary background information, translating, and editing the folktales she had collected. When her book, *One Hundred Armenian Tales and Their Folkoristic Relevance,* was published in 1966 by Wayne State University Press, it tied for first place in the University of Chicago Folklore Prize competition.

As Mrs. Villa points out in the Introduction to the present volume, it was in the course of collecting folktales that she became interested in Armenian village life. She made the pilot study for this project in the mid-1960s, and in 1973 she took a sabbatical leave from the Department of English at Oakland Community College in order to undertake the final organization of the materials she had been compiling. In early 1978, however, Mrs. Villa recognized that her failing health would not allow her to complete the manuscript to her own satisfaction, and she therefore submitted it to Wayne State University Press with the hope that it could be finished by a qualified person. She died on October 14, 1978, with the knowledge that her work had been favorably reviewed.

I never had the privilege of meeting Mrs. Villa, but when Dr. Bernard Goldman, the director of Wayne State University Press, proposed that I prepare her manuscript for publication, I read it and recognized its great merit. To mention but one example, the concerns of women—notably child-rearing practices and healing—predominated in her materials. These concerns had been neglected by Soviet Armenian ethnographers, as well as by western anthropologists and specialists in Near Eastern studies; in collecting the information Mrs. Villa had made an important contribution to Armenian ethnography. However, it seemed to me that additional work was necessary to prepare her manuscript for publication. Because of her health, Mrs. Villa had been unable to complete the research required for a comparative study, and she had not consulted the surveys of Armenian ethnography available in Russian and Armenian. Finally, the manuscript needed some reorganization and rewriting.

The reconstruction of the Armenian way of life in this book thus is based on both oral and written sources. In preparing the final version, I have made extensive use of publications by Armenian ethnographers in the Soviet Union, especially those by S. P. Lisit-sian and V. H. Bdoyan. Their work is generally of high quality, broad in scope and careful in inference. It is most useful in the study of Eastern Armenians, and thus complements the recollections of Mrs. Villa's Western Armenian informants, although it also includes data on Western Armenians at the turn of the century. I have also drawn attention to beliefs and practices common to the Armenians and their neighbors, hoping that this eventually will contribute to a deeper explanation of these shared traits. Two aspects of traditional Armenian village culture are particularly interesting. Because they suffered from a shortage of timber and arable soil, the Armenians had to conserve energy and earth. They succeeded, and since they used only renewable resources, they could have perpetuated their way of life indefinitely, had not the violent intrusion of outside forces brought it to a sudden end. Armenian culture exemplifies skill in conserving scarce resources. Furthermore, while the Armenians officially became Christians in 301, many pagan beliefs and rituals persisted in their culture. Armenian attitudes toward nature, beliefs about the evil eye, and many beliefs about the dead owed little to Christianity and probably antedated it. For the historian of religion and the cultural anthropologist, these vestiges of paganism are especially interesting, and I have pointed out these features.

I am indebted to my daughter, Lou Ann Matossian, for reading my manuscript and making many good suggestions for editorial changes.

Mary Kilbourne Matossian
Department of History
University of Maryland

PREFACE

For more than three thousand years, Armenians have inhabited the Anatolian highlands of Asia Minor, struggling to survive in an inhospitable terrain and continually prey to raids and conquest by neighboring peoples. Historical Armenia—as distinguished from an Armenia defined by political boundaries—was, at its greatest expansion, some ten times larger than the present-day Armenian Soviet Socialist Republic. Except for relatively brief and widely separated periods, however, Armenia has not enjoyed the status of an entirely independent national state.[1] This historical Armenia, following a distinction originally made by the Romans, is usually divided into Greater Armenia, lying east of the Euphrates River, and Lesser Armenia, to the west of it; the total area includes modern northeastern Turkey, the Armenian Soviet Socialist Republic, and part of the Azerbaijan region in northwest Iran. Near the center, roughly midway between the two great lakes of Van and Sevan, looms Mount Ararat, traditionally the landing place of Noah's Ark and a focal point for awe and worship since prehistoric times.

The rugged Armenian homeland produced a civilization strongly marked by its environment. Although the Ararat Plain and certain other areas are fertile, the growing season is short and adequate rainfall uncertain. Mountain-dwellers, in particular, had to come to terms with stony soil and long, severe winters. Moreover, individual communities frequently were so isolated from each other by geographical features that contacts with other villages were rare. From such conditions evolved a conservative farming and stock-

breeding culture, characterized by self-reliance, a strongly patriarchal social organization, and a tenacious clinging to family and
community ties in the face of hostile natural forces and human
adversaries. It seems somehow typical of the Armenians that their
country was the first to adopt Christianity as a state religion at the
end of the third century, and that within the next one hundred
years they had rejected external authority and made their church
autonomous.[2]

Nevertheless, self-reliance and self-sufficiency have not been
enough to protect the Armenians from political subjugation. From
very early in their history, the Armenians have shared their pla-
teau with the Kurds, a group ethnically and linguistically related to
the Iranians; Kurdish raids and competition for summer pastures
were ever-present features of Armenian life. The Kurds, however,
did not attempt organized conquest or political oppression. That
was left to the governments of neighboring countries and empires.
Again and again, part or all of Armenia was conquered: through
the fourteenth century, the list of rulers includes the Persians,
Romans, Byzantines, Arabs, Mamelukes, Seljuk Turks, and the
Mongols under Tamerlane, who not only subjugated Greater Armenia but also massacred much of the population. When Tamerlane died in 1405, the Ottoman Turks seized the opportunity to
invade Armenia, and by the sixteenth century it was entirely in
their hands. Turkey and Persia (modern Iran) continued to dispute
possession of Eastern Armenia; it was from Persia that Russia
eventually acquired, in 1828, what is now Soviet Armenia.

Ottoman authority meant that the Christian Armenians had to
endure discrimination and sometimes outright persecution, but an
increasing number of those with the opportunity and means became traders, merchants, and financiers. The majority of the rural
population, however, continued to live much as they had always
done. Yet the Armenians as a whole maintained a strong sense of
national identity. Some assimilation to the majority culture did of
course occur, particularly in those areas where the pressures of
social and economic discrimination were most intense. In Western
Armenia, for example, by the latter half of the nineteenth century
the Armenian town-dwelling population in Adana, Caesarea, Ain-

tab (now Gaziantep), and Tokat had begun to speak only Turkish. However, with the founding of many Christian missionary Armenian schools, Armenians could learn or relearn and use the language of their ancestors. In isolated villages, on the other hand, the Armenians not only spoke Armenian, but localized and linguistically conservative dialects of it. This was true, for instance, of Hajin and Kessab. In such cases the school's role was to teach standard literary Armenian.[3]

If the conditions, difficult as they sometimes were, under which the Armenians lived in the first half of the nineteenth century had continued relatively unchanged into the twentieth, it is likely that this book, written by an American-born Armenian in an attempt to capture rapidly vanishing memories of daily life in rural Western Armenia, never would have been undertaken. But a complex chain of action and reaction, ultimately arising from the clash between the ambitious European powers and the Ottoman Empire, had deadly consequences for the Armenians under Turkish rule. As David Lang puts it, "The quarter of a century from 1895 to 1920 was the most tragic in the long and chequered history of the Armenian people."[4] The European powers schemed to divide the territories of the weakened Ottoman Empire among themselves; the Ottoman Turks, who had seen the formerly subjugated Serbs, Romanians, Greeks, and Bulgarians successfully assert a measure of national independence, feared that the Armenians too might attempt to liberate themselves. In any case, the Turks had already lost a significant portion of Armenia that they had previously held to Russia following the war of 1877–78. Armenians had strong ties to the west through American and English Protestant missionary schools within Armenia and the Armenian Catholics' relationship to Rome, and, of course, through business connections as well. The Turkish response was to inflict more hardship and persecution on their Armenian subjects.

Matters came to a head in 1895, when [Sultan Abdul-Hamid II] began to put into effect his "final solution" of the Armenian problem. Special armed troops, called *Hamidiya* after the Sultan, were formed to massacre the Armenian populations in Sassoun, Erzurum, Trebizond, Van, Kharput, Istanbul and Marash. Armenian revolutionaries retaliated by seizing the Ottoman Bank in Istanbul, and appealing to the European powers for help. This was the signal for a general onslaught, in which some 300,000 Armenians perished, and another 80,000 fled to other countries.[5]

When Abdul-Hamid II was toppled by internal revolution in 1908, Armenians supported the so-called Young Turks who replaced him, believing the promises that they would abolish the sultan's oppressive policies and that minority groups would be more justly treated. The truth was horribly different. The ruling junta of the Young Turks revived imperial dreams, and there was no place for Armenians in their vision of a vastly expanded Turkish empire. All of the evidence supports the fact that the Turkish solution to the Armenian question was annihilation of the Armenian population within their reach.[6] This is not the place to retell the events of 1915 and the following years; several of those who survived the massacres, tortures, and death marches have recorded their experiences more effectively than I could do.[7] The consequence, however, was that approximately 1.5 million men, women, and children—half of the Turkish Armenian population—died, either killed outright, maltreated and left to perish, or victims of exposure and starvation as they tried to flee to Russian-held Armenia or other countries. Every trace of Western Armenian culture could have been destroyed; that it was not is a tribute to the courage and almost incredible endurance of those who escaped and carried their traditions with them.

I have attempted to capture and preserve, however incompletely, the myriad details of daily living in rural Western Armenia before World War I and the large-scale massacres began. My informants often were individuals with some social standing in their own communities, but they were not prominent people, important cultural or political figures. In general they were simple and, by modern American standards, minimally educated villagers. The majority of them were women—which reflects the fact that groups of Armenian men were the first to be killed and continued to be imprisoned and murdered in large numbers—and therefore could not know as much of the wider world as their fathers, husbands, uncles, and brothers. Nevertheless, I hope that this book may serve as a memorial to both the victims and the survivors. Without the dead there would have been no need to seek reminiscences thousands of miles away from Armenia, but without these informants' memories, we would know even less of how they lived.

As a child growing up in Delray, an Armenian enclave on the southwest side of Detroit, I often listened to my father reminisce about "the good old days" in his tiny Armenian village. When neighbors dropped in, their visit seldom was complete without my making and serving thick Turkish coffee. After a while one of the men would recall his Old World experiences. Then another would start. So they entertained each other, sometimes for several hours.

At the time, unfortunately, I had little appreciation of the value of their conversations. I only became aware of the scarcity of literature on traditional Armenian village life when I was engaged in the research on Armenian folktales that was incorporated in my *One Hundred Armenian Tales and Their Folkloristic Relevance* (Detroit: Wayne State University Press, 1966). I realized that the sociological insights which the folktales revealed needed to be anchored in studies of the Armenian village family, but I was continually frustrated by the lack of published information. True, there were some sketchy travelogues written by visitors who had passed through the area. The accounts by nineteenth- and early twentieth-century American missionaries were helpful, especially Henry Van Lennep's *Bible Lands: Their Modern Customs and Manners* (New York: Harper, 1875) and two-volume *Travels* in *Little Known Parts of Asia Minor* (London: John Murray, 1870). H. F. B. Lynch's two-volume *Armenia, Travels and Studies* (London: Longmans, Green, 1900, 1901), a rather complete study of part of the Armenian terrain, presents descriptions of the physical characteristics of some of the villages and towns, and there are a few other early accounts of domestic architecture and general information about the Armenian family. However, I was unable to locate much which would enable the present-day student to reconstruct, even in a superficial manner, the life patterns of Armenian villagers at the turn of the twentieth century.

Remembering the conversations of my father and his friends, I wondered if I could draw upon the memories of Detroit Armenians to create a picture of traditional Armenian village life. This would be a delicate task, because the health and the lives of the first-generation Armenians were slipping away. Starting first with five informants, then adding another four, I recorded their recollections, given to me orally in Armenian, and from them developed a partial and exploratory study. Eventually I collected extensive interviews with forty-eight informants, both men and women. The present study is based primarily on the information they provided. The early interviews were transcribed in shorthand, but the later ones are preserved on tapes. Chapter 6 includes some additional material I collected in Delray from 1940 to 1942; the source materials are deposited in the Folklore Archives at Wayne State University. Extensive reading in the literature of the missionaries associated with the American Board of Missions in Turkey has reinforced my findings; there are only a few instances in which the informants' and the missionaries' accounts differed. I have noted these written sources when necessary, and I have also sometimes cited them to provide specific verification of the informants' statements.

Since Armenia was primarily an agricultural land, composed of many, many villages, a few provincial towns, and even fewer large towns, I have concentrated on developing a general description of village life in late nineteenth- and early twentieth-century Armenia. I have not addressed myself to the educated, intellectual, sophisticated life in the towns and provincial capitals. I realize that this study is incomplete, but it is limited, to a very large extent, by the recall of seventy- to eighty-year-old informants, as well as by a shortage of pictures and material artifacts. Most of my informants reached America as refugees from the horrors of the massacres with few, if any, possessions. On the other hand, they came from areas as far east as Van and Georgia and as far west as Bursa village, from as far north as Amasia and as far south as Kessab and Zeitoun. Moreover, I contacted both townspeople and villagers to see if there were significant variations in their life styles. I made every effort to avoid unwarranted generalizations, knowing that because a custom existed in one area it did not necessarily represent the sole Armenian tradition. Having been born and raised in America, I can only imagine the Armenian life outlined here, because I have never seen it. However, I was born into an Armenian family and have lived in a strong Armenian community, and I have thus shared the Armenian values and traditions from my earliest memory.

I appreciate the enthusiastic cooperation of my many informants, as well as the encouragement and direction of Professors Leonard Moss, Esther Callard, and Arnold Pilling of Wayne State University and Dr. William Lockwood of the University of Michigan. I am also grateful to Oakland Community College for the sabbatical in 1973 which facilitated my collecting activity.

Susie Hoogasian Villa

NOTE TO THE TEXT

Armenian words in the text and glossary and Armenian place names have been transliterated to approximate Western Armenian sounds. Diacritical marks have been eliminated. In the Library of Congress system of transcription, Eastern Armenian phonetic values are preferred. In the guide below, however, which is based on the Library of Congress system, the reader will note that the Western Armenian system is preferred, with the Eastern variant in parentheses. This is done to reflect more accurately the pronunciation of the informants from whom Susie Hoogasian Villa collected her oral histories.

The Publisher

Ա	ա	A a
Բ	բ	P p (B b)
Գ	գ	K k (G g)
Դ	դ	T t (D d)
Ե	ե	E e
Զ	զ	Z z
Է	է	E e
Ը	ը	E e
Թ	թ	T t
Ժ	ժ	Zh zh

Ի	ի	E e (I i)
Լ	լ	L l
Խ	խ	Kh kh
Ծ	ծ	Dz dz (Ts ts)
Կ	կ	G g (K k)
Հ	հ	H h
Ձ	ձ	Ts ts (Dz dz)
Ղ	ղ	Gh gh
Ճ	ճ	J j (Ch ch)
Մ	մ	M m
Յ	յ	(Y y)
		H h (at beginning of word)
Ն	ն	N n
Շ	շ	Sh sh
Ո	ո	O o
Չ	չ	Ch ch
Պ	պ	B b (P p)
Ջ	ջ	Ch ch (J j)
Ռ	ռ	R r
Ս	ս	S s
Վ	վ	V v
Տ	տ	D d (T t)
Ր	ր	R r
Ց	ց	Ts ts
Ւ	ւ	W w
Ու	ու	U u
Փ	փ	P p
Ք	ք	K k
ԵՒ	or և	Ev ev
Օ	օ	O o
Ֆ	ֆ	F f

1.

THE VILLAGE COMMUNITY, CLAN, AND HOUSEHOLD

At the end of the nineteenth century, the Armenians were a people without a state, a subject ethnic group clinging to its ancient territory. This territory was divided between the Ottoman and the tsarist empires, and, while each had an official language (Turkish, Russian), most of the rural imperial subjects could not speak it. The central government ruled a heterogeneous collection of peoples; it did not represent a homogeneous body of citizens. In any case, Armenian villagers played no role in political affairs above the local level, although to a large extent they did regulate local affairs according to their own customs. Only when a dispute could not be settled in this way did they turn to higher authorities. The same might be said for each clan and extended family household.

By contemporary western standards, both imperial governments were weak, in that they performed few functions and often could not control the behavior of their subjects even when they tried. Maintaining order in rural areas was especially difficult.[1] The governments were building more roads into the interior and expanding their network of secular courts, but they still could not respond promptly and effectively to civil disturbances. This was evident in 1895 in Anatolia and in 1905 in Transcaucasia, when massacres occurred, in some cases with the participation of local government officials. The principal cause for the governments' weakness was economic. Although commerce and industry were developing at the end of the nineteenth century, most imperial subjects still depended on subsistence agriculture and animal husbandry. The tax base was very limited, and the military needs of the state often exceeded its economic resources. In order to stay strong enough to defend its borders, the state had to include many different ethnic groups under its rule. This ethnic diversity was another cause of weakness, because the various peoples, each rooted in the same territory it had occupied for centuries, resisted assimilation.

Armenian agricultural communities were on a continuum, one end of which was dominated by the central government (especially in the lowland areas) and the other by armed pastoralists, the Kurds (especially in mountainous areas). The placement of a village depended on the water supply, because the people relied mainly on natural springs for drinking water and on streams for irrigation and sometimes sanitation. Well-watered locations often were far apart. The isolated, oasislike character of ovas (alluvial depressions) on the Armenian highland was another factor that forced families to live in compact settlements with minimal contact between neighboring villages. While the arrangement tended to encourage both very intense relationships between the households in one community, it fostered distrust of people in other communities.

The village, highland or lowland, was a collection of households with certain common interests and shared obligations. For example, all villagers had common rights to the use of certain natural resources: water, wild animals and plants, wood, clay, construction stone, lime, and unused land. If the village depended on irrigation, it was the collective responsibility of all households to keep the canals clean and in good repair; the community might hire a village shepherd and night guards for the planted fields. It might pay a traveling barber to cut hair, bleed patients, and pull teeth; it might appoint guardians for orphans and organize a village school. If the central government assessed a tax or other obligation on the village as a whole, it was necessary for the village leaders to divide the load among households.

Village and Family Organization

The general Armenian word for family was *undanik,* which meant a nuclear family consisting of father, mother, and children only. *Ger-*

dastan referred to the extended family clan which could be traced to the same parents or grandparents. The *azk* included many households, not all of them necessarily in the same village. *Ojakh*, "hearth," on the other hand, denoted all of those who shared the same hearth—servants and apprentices as well as blood kin. The ojakh was also a tax unit. A majority of turn-of-the-century Armenians probably lived in nuclear family households. There were times in the family generational cycle when there were no grandparents living and no grandchildren had been born. Sooner or later large extended families broke into segments, and it took time for each segment, in turn, to develop into an extended family household. The shorter the life expectancy of the people in a community, the fewer and smaller were the extended family households.

The village headman usually was a member of the wealthiest and most politically experienced family. If there were a formal election, each candidate presented his hat, which was laid upside-down. Then the male head of each family place a nut or bean into the hat of the candidate of his choice. The villagers paid the headman partly with labor, which they supplied to help his family at harvest time, and partly with gifts of fruit and strong liquor at the New Year and at Easter.

Consulting informally with other influential householders, the headman mediated family and neighbor quarrels, received outside visitors, and distributed the tax load among local families. He could punish offenders with fines, deprivation of freedom, a certain number of blows with a rod (although women were never so punished), and, in extreme cases, exile from the village. With his mediation, clans might settle feuds by intermarriage. In Eastern Armenia, beginning in the latter part of the nineteenth century, the heads of households met in the summer months in the village square to make decisions about village affairs.[2]

The gerdastan, the largest kinship unit among the Armenians, was strongest in those mountainous and subalpine regions of forested areas where peasants privately owned land. There the central government was weakest and the need for self-defense greatest. The principal function of the clan was mutual self-defense. All male members had the duty to avenge any injury done to any clan member. The clan was also strong in newly founded communities in which sentimental ties between unrelated neighbors had not yet developed. It was patriarchal and patrilineal, tracing the relationships through male lines only, and including all descendants from a common ancestor in the male line for six to eight generations. The head of the clan was concerned with all problems involving the honor of the clan, representing it in all disputes over land, mills, and irrigation. He discouraged fraternization between the young people of his clan and those of other clans. Frequently his wife was active as a midwife or healer.

The clan name was derived from the Christian name of the founder, his profession if he were an artisan, or the locality from which he emigrated. Sometimes the name of a woman became the second clan name; in these cases the name was usually that of the founder's wife, who was celebrated for her beauty, wisdom, bravery, and so on. If a male family member took up residence in another village, he was still considered a member of his original clan, but after a clan branch lived in another village for five generations or more, his descendants were considered to be a separate clan, and they used the name of the original male emigrant as their clan name.

Prior to about 1850, only noble families has surnames; after that date individuals tended to adopt a surname (ending in *-ian, -iants, -ints, -unts,* or *-ents*), which was simply the name of the clan to which they belonged. Some clan members formed surnames from the Christian name of the founder of their own branch of the clan. If the legal surname and the clan name of an individual differed, he often used the clan name as supplementary identification.[3]

Clans were exogamous: there was an absolute taboo on marriages between members up to the fourth degree (that is, second cousins could not marry). Although canon law prohibited marriage up to the seventh degree, marriages between third cousins did occur if the clan consisted of only four living generations in a given place. There was also a taboo on marriages with god-kin, and a taboo inside the clan on marriage between a man and his brother's widow.

Clans often occupied a compact piece of territory in a village, which was known as a "quarter" (*tagh*). In Zeitoun, for example, there were four such quarters, bounded by rivers and gorges. Beginning in the early twentieth century, there was more movement, and some quarters no longer were composed entirely of the households of members of one clan. However, since clan members lived close by, they often found it convenient to form economic units entirely from blood relatives. For example, cooperative plowing units and dairying associations frequently were made up only of clan members. In addition, a single clan might own certains kinds of property: forested tracts, mills, olive presses, and slow-growing trees, especially nut trees. The whole clan had to give its consent to the disposal of any clan property.[4]

The Armenian clan, therefore, resembled clans that could be found in both rural and urban parts of Italy, Germany, and southern France in the fourteenth and fifteenth centuries. A similar institution also was current in the late nineteenth and early twentieth centuries among the Turks, Abkhazians, Georgians, Hungarians, Serbs, Macedonians, Albanians, and Greeks. Among those peoples too, clans often were associated with a particular territory within a settlement. They were exogamous through the second-cousin relationship. Members also defended each other in case of a feud.[5] Probably the strength of clan loyalty varied inversely with the strength of the central government: the weaker that government, the stronger the clan.

It was customary to obtain the consent of the clan leader before a clan member married. The entire clan would attend the wedding, participating in the rituals and bringing presents. This was true even if clan members lived in a different community from that of the bride or groom. Armenian clans often buried their dead in a special clan area in the local cemetery, or even in a special clan cemetery. The clan leader was responsible for the care of trees, plants, and vegetables grown in the clan plot.

Some clans had special cult centers: at a holy tree in the clan cemetery, or a holy ojakh, a little chapel in the corner of a house. This might be in an occupied home that was considered to be especially lucky, or in the abandoned house of an ancestor. In this ojakh there might be candlesticks for candles brought by devotees, prayerbooks, gospels, a cross, family talismans, and votive objects such as rags and wax or iron figures, representing the body of a sick person for whose health a visitor had prayed. Newlyweds might come to this ojakh after their church ceremony to receive the blessing of a happy home.[6]

The Armenian extended family, the gerdastan, usually consisted of several generations, comprising fifteen to fifty persons, living under the same roof. However, in Western Armenia, especially in isolated mountainous areas such as Sassoun, the gerdastan might include five to six generations and seventy to one hundred persons. In Western Armenia the strength of this institution lasted up to World War I, largely because of the physical insecurity which the Armenians felt. In Eastern Armenia there was a tendency for the gerdastan to divide earlier: the married sons, having remained with their parents while their children were still young, formed separate households when their children were older.[7]

The gerdastan was the principal economic productive unit, a tax unit, and of course the place where children learned the most essential lessons of their lives. It was customary for all adults in the household to reprimand children when they misbehaved. The gerdastan, like the clan, was patriarchal and patrilineal. The marriage of its members was normally patrilocal; that is, the wife moved into the household of her husband and his parents. In these respects, the gerdastan was like the ancient Roman *familia,* the Serb, Albanian, Macedonian, and Bulgarian *zadruga,* and the Russian *bol'shaia sem'ia (pechishche, dvorishche).*[8] All household property was communal except articles of personal use, weapons, artisans' tools, certain horses, and the dowry and jewelry of the women.

Armenians probably maintained this form of family organization in response to two circumstances. The first was physical insecurity, especially in rural areas. The more isolated the settlement, the larger the gerdastan. People wanted their closest relatives to be on hand in case of raids and persecutions. The gerdastan would care for the wives and children of men active in local feuds. The second circumstance was the high rate of child mortality. It was customary for girls to marry soon after puberty in order to have maximum time in which to produce children. A thirteen-year-old girl and her young husband were not usually able to run an independent household, however. Sometimes the young husband had to work outside the village. It made sense for them to live with the husband's parents, married brothers, and unmarried sisters.

The division of functions in the gerdastan was based on two principles: age and sex. Older people had correspondingly greater authority, so long as they were mentally and physically fit. Because males were dominant over females, the senior male member was the head of the family (*nahabed, dahnooder*). He was responsible for maintaining the family honor by disciplining its members, and he represented the family in all negotiations with outsiders. His powers included the right to disinherit and expel disobedient offspring. When he died, his eldest son usually replaced him.

The wife of the family head (*dahn deegeen*) administrated the everyday operations within the household. She had the keys to the storeroom and supervised food and fiber processing. She was also in charge of all child rearing, having more authority over a child than either of its parents. She settled or prevented quarrels between household members and tried to eliminate influences that brought division or loss to the household. The head of household did not consult his wife on political and commercial matters, but he did consult her in decisions concerning the marriages of their children. She had the greatest influence in a decision involving the marriage of a daughter, and would often consult her brother. After the death of her husband, the wife of her eldest son usually replaced her.

The eldest son usually looked after the domestic animals. Another son directed field work at sowing and harvest time. The wife of the eldest son supervised domestic life when her mother-in-law was absent.

The folding together and storage of bedding in the morning symbolized the unity of the household. When a family group within the household folded its bedding separately, the neighbors would say that the household was "pregnant"—that it would soon divide. However, in Western Armenia a household usually did not divide until the death of the male head and his wife.

If both parents were dead, the eldest son inherited the paternal homestead. If the mother were alive, the household would usually go to the youngest son. Normally all property was divided equally among brothers; in some places unmarried daughters received a half-share. The dowry of the mother and her personal earnings were hers to dispose of as she wished, and were not included in the paternal household property. Sometimes the village headman and the priest helped in the division of the property. There would be a ceremony at the time of division, during which the founder of a new household took some fire from the paternal hearth to light the fire in his own.[9]

If the father died before the grandfather, the father's family cared for the widow and her children. If the widow remarried or found a job in town, she might take the children with her. According to Informant 15, from Zeitoun, in some areas when the grandfather died the father's share of the inheritance did not go to his children. When a family had no sons, they might marry a daughter to a poor young man (*dahn pesah*), who would come to live in her household and inherit from her father. The Armenians did not consider this kind of marriage normal; it was demeaning to the man.

There was especially great respect for the *gunkahyr* ("godfather") in the Armenian tradition; some informants indicated that it was even greater than that given to parents. A number of the Detroit informants said that the godfather must not be a blood relative (Informants 4, 21, 25, 39, 43), but, on the other hand, Informant 27, from Malatia, identified the godfather as the father's sister's son.

With few exceptions, the man who served as godfather to one child in a family was also godfather to all of the other children born into the household. The role was inherited, being passed from father to oldest son, so that for generations one family furnished the godfather for all baptisms and for the weddings of all male children of another family. One informant said that his gunkahyr family had held that relationship for over one hundred years, and only three of the entire group of Detroiters indicated that the godfather for an individual's baptism could be anyone that the family selected (Informants 3, 29, 43). According to Informant

8, if it happened at some time that the designated godfather family had no sons, a daughter's husband often held the child at the christening. If two families exchanged the godfather function, the role was known as *khachi gunkahyr* or *khach kavor* (Informants 12, 16, 25, 26). Informant 22 added that the godfather position could not be changed without the consent of the godfather himself. This might become necessary if the godfather's entire family moved to another country—America, for example.

There were also certain taboos connected with the godfather-godfamily tie. In the *khachi gunkahyr* relationship, marriage between the families was prohibited even though they had no blood ties (Informants 13, 48). Informant 4 said that the *sanahyr*, the father of the child that received the services of the godfather, must not walk on the roof of the godfather's house. Informant 25 remembered that when her grandmother made bread in the godfather's house, she did not sit on the cushion next to the oven, but instead, as a sign of respect, removed her apron and sat on that.

Domestic Architecture

Typically, villages in Eastern and Western Armenia were laid out somewhat differently. In Western Armenia, where physical insecurity was greater, the people constructed their buildings flush with each other. Home, stables, and sheepfold were often interconnected. The homes of neighbors might adjoin, and there might be openings in the dividing walls between dwellings through which people, food, and messages could pass. Thus a village might be a kind of labyrinthine, semiunderground warren in which people could hide themselves and their valuables.[10] A similar way of building a settlement, evidently for defensive reasons, was employed by the people of Çatal Hüyük, entral Anatolia, in the seventh to sixth millennia B.C.[11] In the east, where there was more security, the dwelling and service buildings were more often separated and the households farther apart, especially on the level ground. In some villages the flat roofs of the houses were contiguous, forming an area for communal activities; in others, these activities took place in the churchyard or an open square. Orchards were at the edge of the village, as was the cemetery, which was often located on an elevated spot. Still farther out were the cultivated fields. Ethnographers never mention any Armenian family living in an isolated farmstead away from a village.

As a rule, turn-of-the-century Armenian villages were small. August von Haxthausen, who published an account of his midcentury travels in the area, observed that lowland Armenian villages usually contained two to three hundred houses, while mountain communities consisted of twenty to thirty farms.[12] The population probably had decreased by the end of the century and continued to decline into the first years of the new one, as massacres, famine, and continued emigration by Armenians seeking safety and opportunity took their toll. In the smallest villages or in those which had been destroyed by various raids and had not been rebuilt, often only homes and the village church and school were to be found. More well-to-do villages had stores selling dry goods and general items, which sometimes were located on the first floor of a family residence. Some of these stores were owned by individual families, some by the church. In larger villages, the "town square" was considerably developed, having a blacksmith, a smith who cleaned and repaired copper utensils, and frequently a butcher in addition to the general stores.

Taking both Eastern and Western Armenia into account, it may be said that houses typically were tightly clustered, often abutting on two or even three sides, and with the side facing the street protected by a high, mud-brick wall. Behind the wall was an open courtyard, called either a *pag* (Armenian) or *dord* (Turkish), which often was partly paved with flat stones. Flowers, vegetables, and fruit-bearing trees might grow there; domestic animals moved about in a section reserved for them, and some householders also kept beehives. There was often a fireplace in the courtyard for heating water for summer bathing and laundry. The lowest level of the dwelling contained the *maran*, a storeroom where the family kept grain, dried fruits, and other foodstuffs.

In some cases a villager excavated a hillside and roofed over the dug-out area. Both Informant 39, from Hajin, and Informant 41, from Karakehoy, near Adana, mentioned such houses; the latter said that his own house was built on the slope of a hill in such a way that the front entrance was level with the street and the hillside formed the back of the house. One had to step up from the hill to reach the roof, and even then one could climb onto it only from the back.

Village houses usually were constructed of small mud bricks or larger bricks called *kerpeech*.[13] These were made of mud and fine clay, which were mixed together, poured into molds, and left to dry in the sun. Where there was a supply sufficient to start the building, the bricks were lined up to form a wall and mortared with mud. After the outside of the dwelling was completed, a mixture of black mud and fine straw was applied to the surface as a sealer. Informant 13, from Akor village in Kharpert province, who worked as a plasterer, described another method of finishing used in mountainous areas. A large piece of limestone was heated for at least twenty-four hours (on one occasion this informant spoke of three days and three nights), until it crumbled. The resulting powder was then mixed with straw and water, sometimes including a small amount of blueing; when spread over the outside walls, this mixture formed a hard and durable surface.

Other dwellings were built of stone over a timber frame, the whole again plastered over with a limestone mixture. Wooden walls normally were found only in the Pontic Mountains and on the northeast shore of the Black Sea, where wood was relatively abundant.[14] Informant 15, from Zeitoun, described the walls of her house as having inner and outer surfaces of wood with an air space about the width of the wood between the two. Tar was poured into the hollow. Whitewash was used for the final finish. Informant 36, from the mountainous Kurdbelem in Gayve district, remembered that her house was made of kerpeech, but pieces of wood were placed over it for added protection on the side of the house exposed to the wind. Typically some wood was used to roof the houses, especially that of the fast-growing poplar; some roofs were tiled.

There were four basic regional variants of the Armenian dwelling:

1. The domed roof dwelling (*aivan, syrah, glkhatun, hatsatun*) was built on the eastern and southern shores of Lake Van and around Moush, areas prone to earthquakes. It was square and had no windows; the principal opening was a *yertik*, or smokehole, in the center of the ceiling.[15] This dark dwelling tended to conserve the maximum amount of heat.

2. The cone roof dwelling was also a windowless square house, found around Erzeroum and Erzunga and in the western Euphrates area. The roof was formed by successive levels of polygonal crowns created from short blocks of wood and also had a central yertik. It too tended to conserve maximum heat.

3. The "grandfather" house (*khoshkh*) was two-story, of varying shapes, and was found in the south, especially in Sassoun, where there was much danger of raiders. This house was similar to a fortress. The lower story had windows and the upper had small openings in the walls for gun barrels. The southern climate being warmer, it had a fireplace with a chimney in the wall instead of a central yertik.

4. The two-story house of varying shapes (rectangular, U-shaped, and others) was found in the warmer horticultural and viticultural regions, such as Erevan, Nakhichevan, Bitlis, and the Van basin. It usually had windows and a flat roof. The Armenians ordinarily covered this roof with a salty earth or sand mixed with clay to bind, which absorbed rainwater and retarded leakage, and kept a stone cylindrical roller called a *logh* on the roof to pack down the earth and press out the water. Village families usually had to use a ladder or outside stairway to get to the roof of such a house, although town houses had inside stairways.[16] Informant 5, from Kharzeet in the Van region, spoke of a permanent stone stairway, strong and wide enough for oxen to climb. But again, this stairway was outside the house.

The typical village house was dark on the inside. Usually the front of the house had no windows or only small ones, placed high up in the wall. Sometimes the back of the house had windows opening on a garden. In a well-to-do village two-story dwelling, the upstairs windows were larger and could usually be moved up and down (Informant 2, from Fenesé, near Caesarea; Informant 25, from Kughee). According to Robert Zouche, oiled paper was more commonly used than glass.[17] Informant 22, from Sepastia, said that some homes were equipped with glass windows and shutters to protect them when the family was away at summer quarters; Informant 12, from Kessab, mentioned windows that had shutters but no glass. Informant 34, from Severeg, the son of a well-to-do craftsman, remembered wide, tall windows protected with iron grillwork.

The stable, or *akhor*, in which the family kept its cattle, horses, and other animals during the winter, was usually rectangular, built of stone, and had a floor paved with stone. In most parts of Eastern Armenia it was dug out of the ground and separated from the dwelling. In Western Armenia the stable was connected with the dwelling and tended to be light, dry, and well constructed. In order to conserve heat, the family might spend its winter evenings in a room adjoining the stable called an *oda*. At other times the oda served as a men's clubroom and place for entertaining guests. The body heat of the animals, together with a fireplace, kept the people warm. Sheep and goats might spend the winter in a special shed called a *gom*.[18]

The Armenians, in order to conserve heat, used a minimum of living space in the winter, and they therefore had to use that space for several different purposes. Consequently, the only fixed furnishing in the rural household, aside from any large storage units, was the *toneer*, a sunken fireplace dug out of the ground to a depth of three to five feet and containing a ceramic cylinder, and perhaps an ojakh. In a very fundamental way, the toneer was the center of the rural Armenian household: it was the symbol of family life as well as the focus of domestic activities, although the published evidence suggests that it had an even greater significance in the past than it had in the villages at the turn of the century. For example, Mardiros Ananikian writes that the new bride, entering her husband's home for the first time, reverently kissed the toneer and, with her husband, piously circled it three times. According to

Manuk Abegian, the bride brought incense from her father's house to burn in her husband's household toneer. The toneer of the village headman served for the observance of marriages and baptisms if the village lacked a church.[19]

Although Detroit informants did not seem to recognize these traditions, certain of their sayings indicate the importance of the toneer. Some of these expressions include: "mookhud chee maree" ("may your smoke not be extinguished"—that is, may your hearth fire, symbol of family life, not die down); "mookhus maretsav" ("my smoke has died down"—that is, I have suffered a calamity); "meguh togh munah vor mehr ojakheen graga vareh" ("let someone remain alive so that he can kindle our hearth and cause the fire to issue forth"—that is, continue the family line). It was around the toneer that people gathered, keeping their hands busy with knitting, carding, or combing wool. Here, too, many ate their food and spread their bedding at night. When the toneer was not being used, it was covered so that children could not fall in, although an American doctor reported that such accidents were not uncommon.[20] In many large households, the fire was rarely extinguished.

An ojakh, on the other hand, seems to have been used much less frequently. Built much like a modern wall fireplace, it was used for cooking, heating water, or for warmth, and might be found in the kitchen area, akhor, pag, or even in individual sleeping rooms in some houses. The *mangal* also could be used for heating or for cooking. It was a type of brazier, a deep earthenware or iron pot with a screen over the opening, handles, and ten- to twelve-inch legs. Finally, a large, heavy comforter could be thrown over a screened-in fire and still provide enough room for several family members to sit under it and be protected against the cold.

The two basic forms of fuel available in Armenia were wood and dried dung. Wood burned longer and, if well seasoned, did not smoke very much; the villagers preferred it for the ojakh, but used it sparingly. Dried dung, called *goashgoor,* burned hotter, but initially smoked a great deal and did not last long. This was often burned in the toneer. The household prepared its supply of goashgoor in the summer, after the animals were released from their winter quarters in the akhor. The accumulated dung was carried to a large pit, where it was mixed with water and, usually, fine straw, although Informant 4, from Vardo-Gundemir, and Informant 43, from Van, indicated that no straw was added. The women used pitchforks or even their bare feet (Informant 18, from Khorsana, near Sepastia) to aerate the mixture, which was then shaped into eight- or nine-inch ovals and placed to dry, one oval overlapping the other, in a sunny place in the pag (Informant 18). Informant 3, from Karaghil, near Moush, Informant 7, from Efgere, and Informant 33, from Shabinkarahisar, near Sepastia, said that the wet goashgoor was stuck to the outside of the house to dry; Informant 41, from Karakehoy, said that sometimes it was dried on the roof.

Pine cones and dried weeds were also gathered and burned in place of scarce wood. Some oil and gas were available, but they were very expensive and were seldom used for fuel. However, gas-burning lamps were placed in niches on the walls, on shelves, or hung from pillars; well-to-do households used oil-burning lamps. Informant 5, from Kharzeet, said that walnuts, which were abundant in his community, were pressed for lamp oil. Some villagers bought candles, while others made their own, using wax from domestic beehives or from wild bees (Informants 4, 5, 11, 15).

Upon entering the main door of a typical village house, a visitor would pass through a wide hallway into the central room, which served as a sitting, sleeping, and dining room. If the house did not contain a separate room for preparing food, one end served this purpose also. The floor usually consisted of packed earth (wood normally was used only on the second story). It was covered, first, with straw matting, and then perhaps with felt or homemade rugs, either flat woven or pile. Frequently the room would have no furniture except a loom, a spinning wheel, several large earthenware jugs in which water was stored, and big wooden chests containing the dowries of the individual women of the household. Often there were also tall chests holding various kinds of grain. Sometimes a *sedeer,* a platform covered with pillows, was built along one wall, but it was not uncommon for families to sit on cushions on the floor or on the floor itself. Well-to-do families had a sedeer on two or three sides of the room, but Informant 11, from Erzeroum, and Informant 46, from Amasia, indicated that only sophisticated and well off households had western-style chairs. Informant 18, from Khorsana, near Sivas, said that even when a family owned several chairs, they did not use them because it was considered *amot* ("shameful") to enjoy such comfort.

When the main room was used as a dining room, the family members sat in a circle on the ground, and a large copper, brass, wood, straw, or earthenware tray heaped with food was placed before them on a stool about two feet high. According to Informant 25, from Kughee, in some areas a quilt was placed over a flat stone on top of the toneer and the tray was placed on it. People ate either with their legs folded under them or stretched out under a comforter. However, Informant 3, from Karaghil, said that people put their dishes right on the ground, which was first covered with a cloth. Informant 15, from Zeitoun, and Informant 41, from Karakehoy, offered the information that in the absence of a tray a family would use a leather mat or a thick tablecloth; other families used the cloth in which the bread for their meal had been wrapped. Some persons criss-crossed or tucked their legs under them while eating; others knelt on cushions. Informant 26, from Hakusdun, near Kughee, remembered the saying, "Your table should be so low that you will bow to eat." On the other hand, Informant 21, from Meghoozeek, near Erzunga, Informant 27, from Malatia, and Informant 34, from Severeg, said that they sat flat on the floor because they should not be higher than their food. Informant 41 also said that his family ate sitting on the ground because they knelt only in church.

Depending on family finances and the sophistication of the village, individual wooden or earthenware bowls might be available for the diner. Sometimes family members shared bowls if there were not enough to go around. However, in most households each family member had a wooden or metal spoon with which he helped himself from a common dish. Some present-day Armenians, in referring to the size of their household, say, "There were sixty spoons in our household." Bread also might be used as a scoop in place of a spoon. Informant 25 said that forks were unusual except for those who had been to Erzeroum or Constantinople. Both earthenware and china cups were used for drinking.

Sleeping arrangements were equally flexible. Typically, the Armenian village family did not own wooden bedsteads. Family members either stretched out on divans in the oda or on the floor. Each had his own quilted woolen mattress (*doshag*) and a warm comforter which in the morning he folded and put away in a large storage area called a *yukluk*. If there were a number of sleeping rooms in the house, each had its own yukluk; sometimes even part of the food storage area was used for this purpose.

The very complete descriptions provided by the Detroit informants make clear that the construction, layout, efficiency, and furnishings of Armenian village houses varied considerably, depending on their geographical location and the financial and social status of their owners. The following condensed accounts by informants from different villages suggest both the variety of dwellings and something of the kind of daily living that went on in them.

Informant 4, from Vardo-Gundemir: At the entrance to her stone house were heavy pillars that supported a flat roof (*dahneek*) made of logs covered with earth. A hole in the dahneek that could be covered at night afforded ventilation and light. The oda, the main room of the house, was whitewashed, as was the rest of the interior, and had a hard earthen floor. The oda had a wood-burning ojakh against one wall and a toneer in the middle. The house was extended next to the cooking area in order to form a place to store food: various grains in large jars (*petakner*), ground daily as needed; oil and salted cheese; cabbages buried neck-high in dirt to prevent their freezing in the winter; and prepared cubes of ox meat or lamb.

The stone-floored akhor adjoined the house and sheltered all of the family's animals except the sheep, which were guarded by several dogs in the gom, located a short walk away. The gom also served as a place to store fodder. The sheep were taken away to pasture in the summer. At the end of the akhor was a room built for the use of newlyweds or travelers.

In warm weather, bathing and laundry were done in a nearby stream, the family's water supply. The most recently married daughter-in-law fetched the water for household use in a jug carried over her shoulder or on her back. In the winter the family bathed and washed laundry in the akhor. There were no toilets in the house.

The house keys were made of wood and were about ten inches long and three inches wide. The door, however, was never locked.

Informant 5, from Kharzeet: Stone was plentiful around his village and was the main building material. The village houses were attached to each other, either along the side or in back.

His house had a domed dahneek supported by heavy pillars. The dome, made of straw and earth, was only slightly rounded and leveled off to flat sides that extended beyond the walls of the house to shade the ground. There was a hole in the dahneek to let out smoke from the toneer, but there were no other openings. People liked to sit on the flat edges of the roof, and they also used these areas for drying food in the summer.

As one approached the house, he saw a door to the house and one to the akhor. One entered the house into a hall; beyond was the living room with the toneer in the center and a yukluk in the wall. Earthenware or wooden petakner filled with grain were placed along the back wall. There was no outside door to the maran, where pickled vegetables, meat and dairy products, and dried fruits were kept. The informant's family stored quantities of cheese in petakner, which they filled with alternating layers of cheese and salt. Each petak was then tightly covered with a cabbage leaf and buried top side down in the earthen floor. When cheese was needed, a petak was turned upright and the cheese rinsed under water before it was eaten. The informant remarked that the cheese had a poor taste if the container were not inverted for storage. Cottage cheese was stored the same way; fish were salted, but the petak was not turned upside down. Potatoes, turnips, and cabbages were simply buried in the floor.

Cows and horses were kept in the akhor, which also had a special place for chickens at one end. The informant added that there were no donkeys in his village; he had never seen one until he went to Russia. There was a stone-floored area behind the cows for laundry and bathing, but no toilet facilities. Sheep and goats were housed in a gom about two or three city blocks away from the main house. A wall separated the animals from the area where dried grass and other fodder were stored.

The informant said that every village household had a *gahl*, a threshing area. One house had a gahl on the flat roof of the gom and feed storage area, which could be reached by a strong stone stairway outside the house. The oxen were driven up it and made to trample the wheat spread on the roof. When the wheat was broken, the small husks were gathered and kept in the *marak* below to be used for animal feed.

Wealthy families often built an oda or guest house at some distance from their own dwellings. Cows and oxen were kept at one end, separated by a wall from the guest sleeping quarters. A sedeer with pillows was placed against the wall of the sleeping room, and there was either a small toneer or an ojakh for warmth. In the winter the village men would gather in the oda to play cards and tell stories. There were four or five such buildings in the informant's village.

Informant 7, from Efgere: His house, which was built on the rise of a hill, was made of stone and looked down on the roof of the neighboring house, with which it shared one wall. His house was approached from the front through a high stone wall; the pag in front was separated from the street by a wide door in the wall.

The house had three levels. On the first were a kitchen, a living room, and a third room which his family eventually made into an akhor. In order to get to it, the family's one donkey, two horses, and one cow had to walk across the living room.

There were two *toneerner:* one was outside the house and was used for cooking in the summer; the other was in a large hallway. The food storage area was in the basement and could be entered through a trapdoor and stairs from the akhor. One day the donkey fell down these stairs when some member of the household forgot to close the trapdoor.

Informant 17, from Kharadigin: The home of this informant's prosperous family was situated ten to fifteen feet away from the other houses. Kerpeech walls framed her house, which one reached by entering at the street and crossing the courtyard. The front door opened into a living room which ran the full length of the house. This room, which was also used as a place for eating, was separated from the kitchen by a door.

There were two toneerner in the kitchen: a small one for preparing daily meals and a large one for baking. Food was stored next to the kitchen, and fodder in another place behind the kitchen. A kerpeech wall in the latter area screened a large cesspit dug for use as a toilet; a door out of the storage room led into the akhor, which ran the length of the pag. The family bathed and washed laundry in the akhor during the winter when they could not use the river. Another door opened into the akhor from the pag.

In the pag were two toneerner, as well as the stairs that led to the upper level and to the flat dahneek. A large window in the dahneek let light in below. An oda and a "sun room" were added on the second floor when the informant was about eight years old. The men usually gathered in the upstairs oda, while the women grouped themselves downstairs. Sedeer(s) along three walls of the oda were used for sleeping, as was the earthen floor. A separate room housed a spinning wheel and a loom.

Informant 23, from Chengiler: Her three-story kerpeech house was approached directly from the street. At the first-floor entrance was an open pag, from which doors at one side led into the kitchen and a storage area for food. Slightly lower than the first floor was the akhor, which included an elevated area where grapes were squeezed. The juice ran down into basins and then into barrels. The strong alcoholic drink called *rakhee* was also made in the akhor.

On the other side of the open pag, protected from the entrance, was the place where one sat to be bathed. Once a month the family went to a Turkish bath. Nearby rivers were used for laundry; washed clothes were spread out on bushes and quickly dried.

Although food was prepared in the kitchen, it was eaten in a large center room on the second floor, which was reached by a wooden stairway. Food supplies were also stored in chests along one wall of this large living area; bedding was stored in a yukluk along another. This room opened into two abutting rooms, each heated by an ojakh. The family slept there in the winter, but in the summer they slept in the back courtyard, where walnut, date, pistachio, and chestnut trees grew.

Jutting out of the house on the second floor was a wood-enclosed toilet with a wooden seat. Waste dropped to the ground where it was buried. The rags used for wiping were burned.

For a small fee, the women could use the communal oven in their tagh. On every street was a fountain for drinking.

Informant 38, from Chanakjee: His house was built at street level, but one had to climb several steps to reach the front door, which was set higher than the two large doors of the akhor. His animals entered the akhor after ascending a slight incline that began below street level. Family members used the akhor as a toilet as well as a place to bathe. The stone roof of the akhor was strongly reinforced to support the weight of the stabled animals or of the family members who slept there in warm weather.

The main roof of the structure could be reached from the akhor by an inside stairway or by outside stairs made of hard earth. There was a large window on the roof through which one could enter the house. Like the windows on the akhor level, it admitted light and fresh air. The rest of the house was made of stone, except for the second-level floor, which, though made of earth, was as hard as cement.

In the main room on the higher level of the house was an ojakh for cooking and a heating stove. Sedeer(s) were sometimes placed along the walls and, since this room was used for sleeping, bedding was stored in a yukluk. From this room a door led to a long narrow maran, where the preserved foods and dairy products were stored. On the other side of the maran was another room used for sleeping; beyond it was the toneer.

Informant 39, from Hajin: The village streets were straight, with houses on both sides. Because of the mountainous terrain, the roof of one house might be level with the next street. Under each house was an akhor and place where wood was kept. The toilet was in the akhor. A mound of earth was built, and a place to sit was provided; whoever used the toilet threw in a shovel of dirt. When the mound became too smelly, it was covered and a new mound started. Bathing was done with the aid of large copper basins, and most families went to the Turkish bath once a month.

The informant's ancestral home had been divided among three brothers. It was an incomplete division; they lived like one big family but had to go out a door to get into another part of the house. Each family cooked its own food and raised its own children. However, there were cubby holes in the walls which served as passages between the families, so that communicating was easy. Thus they were separate yet unified.

One entered her grandfather's house into a main hall with three adjoining rooms. Two steps led to a small cave, which was where her uncle's book-filled study was located. This room was kept as though it were a shrine. Her uncle, the oldest child of the oldest brother, had left for Paris at the age of fifteen and had returned only once for a short visit. There was a large living room. A wood-burning ojakh in one corner kept most of the house warm in winter and was also used for cooking.

The village households did not have toneerner. Instead, women took their flour to public ovens, where they kneaded the dough in wooden troughs and set it to rise. They returned to shape the dough and bake it. Each family had a special emblem which they used to identify their loaves. Each family contributed wood for the huge ovens; the owner was paid in bread.

2.

DAILY LIFE

To a large extent, each Armenian village family was self-sufficient, producing all or most of its food and clothing and many of its tools and furnishings. The most essential Armenian foods were grain, dairy products, vegetables, and fruits. Most rural folk considered animals too valuable to use for meat, except in small quantities and on special occasions. This was a conservationist strategy, since it was more economical to eat grain directly than to feed it to animals and then eat them. In addition, cows, sheep, and goats on the hoof yielded milk; chickens produced eggs; cattle provided traction power; sheep provided wool.

For the rest of its needs, the typical village family resorted to barter. Highland families gave salted butter, cheese, and wheat to lowland families in exchange for olives, fruits, and nuts. The more affluent peasant families could obtain shoes, fabric, and metal objects from village and town artisans. However, village artisans were not full-time specialists, and they themselves engaged in part-time agriculture and animal husbandry. Life was marked by self-sufficiency, frugality, and the need to work for a common goal.

Agriculture and Animal Husbandry

By tradition, men did the work of plowing and sowing grain in "Mother Earth." Probably this practice was based on a sexual analogy, since men were bearers of seed and to all appearances women were not. The male monopoly on plowing and sowing probably originally had magical significance and was thought to contribute to the fertility of the soil; it was widespread in Europe and the Near East.[1] In any case, western observers commented that Armenians still employed the same kind of implements as had been used two thousand years before. For example, the hoe was a stick about two feet long, and very awkward and heavy. A man had to bend almost to the ground as he used it.[2] The spade was somewhat more efficient. It had a handle longer than a man is tall, with a bit of wood upon which the foot was set in order to force the sharp blade further into the ground. The length of the handle enabled the laborer to place his whole weight on it, thereby using the spade as a lever to raise a large quantity of soil.

Armenians used two kinds of plows: the *aror,* or scratch plow, made of a tree branch and usually having a metal share; and the *gutan,* or heavy plow, which was usually wheeled and had a metal share, coulter, and moldboard. They used the aror on light, dry, upland soils and the gutan on wet, alluvial lowland soils. It took four to twelve pairs of oxen or water buffalo to pull the gutan, and often families had to combine resources, forming the plowing cooperative unit called a *hamkal* or *harakash.* Frequently all of the members of a hamkal were kinsmen. Five to eight plowmen worked with the animals over a twenty-five to forty-day period, often sleeping overnight in the fields. Both adults and children collected the loose stones and piled them beside the fields, believing that such cairns made the soil fertile.[3]

Seed was sown broadcast, except in the arid Van basin, where it was sown in rows to conserve moisture. (The Armenians of the Van basin were the only Near Eastern people to employ this advanced agricultural technique before the beginning of the twentieth century.)[4] They fertilized their fields with ashes, animal dung, and human excrement. The ashes served to alkalize the soil and the excrement fertilized it effectively.[5]

The standard vehicle used in Armenia at the turn of the century was the two-wheeled cart, fitted either with solid or with spoked wheels. One with solid wheels was called a "blind" cart (*guyr sail*).

To keep it from squeaking too much, people placed flour on the axle. Four-wheeled vehicles were used only in Shirak and the Ararat Plain. The villagers hitched oxen or asses to their carts, using horses only for riding and carrying light goods to market.[6]

Cereals were the staple crops among the Armenians. The particular crops grown of course varied by area, but wheat was of major importance throughout the country. Informants 3, 4, and 5, from the Moush area, spoke of four different kinds of wheat. Armenians preferred to eat the wheat they grew, growing barley for animal fodder. They also grew millet, rye, corn, and rice.

The quantities and types of other agricultural products also varied by area, but the group of informants spoke of a wide range of vegetables, fruits, and nuts. Villagers grew vegetables in a garden plot and might have small orchards; a householder's vineyard was planted at some distance from the village, side-by-side with his neighbors' vineyards. The grape, grown during the warm dry summer in the east and south, was the most important single fruit crop. The climate was too cold for citrus fruits.

Informants 5, 24, and 43, from the Van region, mentioned chick peas, beets, okra, fava beans, cucumbers, tomatoes, lentils, potatoes, *gangar* (a vegetable similar to artichoke), turnips, and cabbage. Walnut, almond, and hazelnut trees were commonly grown. These villagers also grew tobacco and a few opium plants, and Informant 43 added that opium, greatly diluted with water, was sometimes used to relieve pain, even for children. Informant 21 said that in Erzunga, in addition to much wheat and barley, there were watermelons, beans, and cucumbers. Cotton and hemp were grown for yarn and thread, but these villagers did not grow tobacco. There were no nuts, but there were mulberry, apple, plum, apricot, pear, cherry, and quince trees.

In the Moush area, according to Informants 3, 4, and 45, there were quantities of pumpkins, squash, cabbage, beets, peppers, and beans. Flax was also grown, as much for its oil as for its fiber. However, Informant 4 observed that fruit was scarce in some villages because they had no orchards. Informant 29 said that several kinds of wheat, barley, and corn were staples in Kughee village, where the inhabitants also grew beans, beets, cucumbers, eggplant, squash, pumpkin, cabbage, and flax; their orchards provided apples, apricots, plums, pears, and mulberries. The Kessab region, according to Informant 12, produced chick peas, okra, eggplant, potatoes, onions, green beans, apples, dates, and grapes.

Informants 29 and 20 mentioned the rich orchards of the western regions near Constantinople; in the Bursa area, according to Informant 23, there were olive, date, plum, walnut, chestnut, pistachio, and quince trees, as well as abundant crops of artichokes, lima beans, black-eyed peas, and tomatoes. Informant 44, from the Caesarea region, remarked only on the fields of wheat, barley, and corn, but certainly at least some of the crops familiar to other parts of Armenia were also grown there.

The villagers supplemented their cultivated produce in several ways. Those who lived in mountainous areas gathered wild greens, which they braided, dried, and then stored for animal feed (Informants 3, 4, 5, 41, 45). Informant 3 said that villagers in the Moush area also used some of these greens in preparing food for their households, especially in combination with eggs or cheese. The greens were substituted for spinach or Swiss chard. Where forests remained they found bear, foxes, and deer; elsewhere there were partridge, quail, wild ducks, and geese. The Armenians also prized certain lake fish, the *ishkhan tzoog* of Lake Sevan and the *tarekh* of Lake Van. The production and sale of salt was a government monopoly in the Ottoman Empire, but Informant 9, from Govdun, near Sepastia, said that some Western Armenians collected it for themselves. They would make a hollow in the ground, fence it with boards, flood it, and then let the water run off slowly, leaving the salt behind. Thus, salt came from Mother Earth. Perhaps this was why some Armenian peasants stored salt in ceramic cellars in the shape of a female.

A typical Armenian village family might raise cattle, sheep, or goats. The family obtained most of the protein, calcium, and vitamins in its diet from the milk of its goats, sheep, or cattle, and their care and feeding was an important element in daily life. In the winter the livestock shared the domestic buildings with the family; in the summer the herds often were moved to pastures at higher elevations, where the rain kept the grass green. This was an economical practice, because it freed the scarce arable land for the production of plant foods. The village community might divide, with many of the women accompanying the animals to summer pasture in order to process the milk on the spot.

If a cattle herdsman were hired, his work began at the spring equinox and ended at the fall equinox. Sheep, however, might graze outdoors all year long, and were cared for somewhat differently. If a family had many sheep, it had a shepherd of its own, a role frequently filled by a woman. Informant 13, from Akor village in Kharpert province, pointed out that the villagers believed that it was wrong to eat an animal which had died of natural causes, and so a shepherd had to become something of an expert at knowing when an animal should be killed in order to avoid the taboo. According to Informant 4, from the village of Vardo-Gundemir, near Moush, it was believed that a good shepherd could control his sheep by playing the flute. With one tune he could send the sheep to the edge of a river, and with another he could stop them from drinking. Informant 5, from Kharzeet, Van region, said that in some places sheep were branded on their noses, while other animals were branded on the flank. In other areas, special cuts were made in the sheeps' ears (Informant 38, from Chanakjee village, near Kughee).

Because they prized honey as a sweetener for their confections and ritual dishes, some Armenians kept bees, especially in forested areas such as Lori, Zangezur, Sassoun, and Zeitoun.[7] Informants 19, 26, 29, and 38 also spoke of enjoying the sweet substance called *manana* ("manna"; probably the lichen *Lecanora esculenta*, commonly called cup moss[8]), which they collected from plants and bushes. (According to Informant 5, manana appeared only on oak trees.) Informants 4 and 45 described manana as white, similar in appearance to salt, but sticky. People broke off branches bearing the manana and dried them in the sun; the dried pieces were then packed into jars and used as sugar if honey were not available. The manana could also be eaten as candy or boiled for syrup.

Harvesting and Food Processing

Anticipating the long, hard winter, the Armenian village family worked throughout the summer and fall, preparing foodstuffs for the time when, together with their animals, they would remain indoors, clinging to the warmth and safety of their homes until the spring. Field work was normally a male task, while food preparation and storage was alloted to the women, but the Detroit informants have made clear that many women worked in the fields beside the men when extra help was needed in the harvest season. Additional workers might also be hired from neighboring villages (Informant 24). The harvesters worked with sickles and scythes, and, according to Informant 43 from Van, they believed that they would not have enough strength to perform such heavy labor unless the *pilaf,* the rice- or wheat-based meals served to them in the fields, had so much butter that it would run to their elbows when they scooped up the food with pieces of flat bread.

After harvesting, the wheat was threshed on the gahl. Some families owned their own gahl, but more frequently families hired the use of a large threshing area owned by some well-to-do man. Some of the early published sources describe the threshing process, which commonly involved a wooden frame equipped with a drag spiked with flint teeth or fitted with stones.[9]

> Horses or oxen are harnessed to it and driven round and round . . . several people standing on the machine the while to give it weight. The process goes on until not only is the [grain] threshed but the straw is chopped fine like chaff. When the grain has been winnowed and washed, it is spread out to dry before being stored. The chopped straw is used as food for the horses and cattle which are fed upon it almost entirely. It is stored in heaps, plastered over thickly with mud.

Both men and women worked to winnow the grain by throwing it into the air with shovels.

After winnowing, some of the grain was sent to a mill to be ground into flour; the rest was processed at home. Sometimes the women used whole grain to make a special ritual porridge called *hadig*. More commonly, however, after removing the chaff and impurities by sifting and washing, they boiled the wheat, dried it, and broke it into groats, called *bulgher*, by beating it with sticks or grinding it with stone grinders. Frequently, neighborhood women met and helped each other, one pouring the grain into the stone mill while two or three others guided the grinding hand. Then the bulgher was put through several screens to sort it according to size, the coarser pieces to be used in various cereal mixtures and the finer pieces to be mixed with meat. Although almost all of the female informants indicated that they ground the bulgher within days after the harvest, Informant 4, from Vardo-Gundemir, said that it was ground as it was needed. After processing, wheat and other cereal crops were poured into tall, upright chests. These containers were equipped with openings at the bottom so that the lowermost deposit, which was most exposed to damp, could be used first.

Wheat which was to be used for flour was not boiled, but simply washed, dried, checked for impurities, and taken to be milled. The farmer paid a fee to the miller for the use of his equipment (Informant 22). If a village was lucky enough to have a mill nearby, well and good. Otherwise, the wheat had to be taken to the nearest large town. Informant 26 from Hakusdun, near Kughee, said that while she was in the village, a mill was finally established for village use. Before that the villagers traveled to Erzeroum, a two-day walk.

One of the most important uses for the milled flour was to make the large quantities of bread consumed by the average Armenian household. When baking was to be done at home, a good fire was laid in the family toneer, and when it became red-hot, the bread-baking crew started to work. Using large flat stones as working areas, one woman rolled out the dough with a rolling pin, while another slapped it against the hot sides of the toneer with a trowel. Sometimes the leavened dough was patted, not rolled. The entire circumference of the toneer was used for the baking. When the circle was completely lined with dough, the first ovals were ready to remove. The heat was so intense that the baker wrapped her face, head, and arm including her hand to prevent burning herself as she bent over. Some older women, particularly widows, made their living going from one place to another, baking toneer bread.

In smaller homes, a single bread-baking event produced tall piles of this thin, pancake-shaped bread, known as *lavash* or *dahn hatz,* which, covered with a clean cloth, could be stored for months ahead on wooden shelves, often suspended from the ceiling. When it was to be eaten, the bread was dampened slightly with water to make it pliable. In villages where there were large extended families, lavash was made every day. Informant 3, from Karaghil, said that in these homes the newest daughter-in-law had the responsibility of placing a large jar of water in the toneer each night so that the women had warm water for bread-making in the morning. Other villagers indicated that baking was done three times a week.

Sometimes, if bread were needed in a hurry, women made *sadj hatz;* Informant 15, from Zeitoun, and Informant 41, from Karakehoy, mentioned that in several areas villagers actually preferred it to lavash. The dough for sadj hatz was rolled very thin, to the size of a "half table"—in other words, to about eighteen inches in diameter. Often women made enough for two or three months' use, folding and piling it up "to the height of a man." As it was needed, the sadj hatz was dipped into water to freshen it and make it sufficiently pliable that it could be used to scoop up other foods.

Women from some of the more prosperous large villages spoke of sending bread dough out to be baked. Some households also sent out the prepared dough for pastries and other baked goods (Informants 2, 20). Informant 10, from Caesarea, Informant 12, from Kessab, and Informant 34, from Severeg, spoke of public ovens located on various streets. Informant 12 added that the public oven had been built by the people in that tagh. Although anyone could use it, she had to notify others ahead as to when she would need it and take her own fuel, dried weeds from the mountains. Finished with her baking, she filled her now empty dough pan, covered it with a cloth, and carried the baked bread home on her shoulder or her head.

Informant 39, from Hajin, described the procedure in areas where the community oven was privately owned and the individual user paid the owner a fee. The dough was mixed at the oven and set to rise. The woman returned to shape it, using her own special emblem which identified her bread. Then she baked it and carried it home in her bread trough.

Dairy products of various kinds also played an important role in the Armenian diet. Almost immediately after milking, women boiled the milk, after which they churned or cultured it. From churning they obtained butter and buttermilk; from culturing, yogurt (*madzoon*) and cheese. All of these products eventually were stored in earthen vessels in the maran, but they required processing in a variety of ways. For example, some households which needed a great quantity of butter used the skin of an animal—usually that of a goat—as a churn (Informant 13, from Akor village, and Informant 39, from Hajin). The hairy hide was removed, the skin membrane washed carefully and sweetened, and the legs were tied tightly. Only one opening was left, usually at the neck. It was then hung with strong rope from a wall or the rafters. Madzoon was poured into it, the opening was tied, and the churn was shaken gently.[10] When the desired quantity was prepared, the skin was slashed, the butter removed, melted to remove impurities, salted, and poured in earthenware jars for storage. Usually such a procedure provided enough butter for most households for the winter.

Women in other areas described a churn which was a long earthenware shaker, often red in color, narrow at each end and wide in the center, and with a hole on the top. The churn was held at chest height and moved back and forth; others rested the churn on a pillow and tilted it repeatedly. When the butter was ready, it was placed in a pan of cold water, squeezed dry, salted, and packed into earthenware containers (Informants 4, 43, 45). Informant 12 described an unusual earthenware churn with three handles, one of which was placed on the floor and the other two used to shake the container.

Informant 3, from Karaghil, remembered a song which the women sang as they moved the household churn back and forth.

Kunnotz keshdem—
I'll make butter.

I'll give the butter to Hagop;
I'll give the cheese to Margose.

Kunnotz keshdem—
I'll make butter.
I'll give the butter to Hagop;
I'll give the madzoon to Toros;
From the first grain's liquid's
    liquid, I'll give to Margose.

There were several other processes for making dairy foods. Informant 9, from Govdun, near Sepastia, and Informant 18, from Khorsana village, near Sepastia, said that some women poured madzoon into large bags and weighted them down to remove the water. The remaining curds were shaped into balls, dried on the dahneek, and then stored. Informant 5, from Kharzeet, described another type of dairy food made of cottage cheese, butter, and green onions.

Baghsgutahn was made by boiling *tahn*, a drink made from madzoon and water, and letting it sour. After it was put into cloth bags to drain, the remaining curds were stored in earthenware containers. Another dairy product was made by putting salt on madzoon and straining it to remove the liquid. Then it was shaped and stored in earthenware vats without drying. Informant 9 mentioned another method, in which tahn was poured into a porous earthenware container. The liquid evaporated until only a thick madzoon-like substance remained, which was then stored for the winter. Informant 15, from Zeitoun, said that it was placed on sheets on the white rocks of the mountain, where it dried in a week and was stored. Still another recipe required madzoon and whole wheat. These were kneaded together with salt and spearmint. Then they were shaped into finger-sized pieces and placed on the dahneek to dry. *Surkik*, was made with dry cottage cheese. First shaped into balls, it was then coated with black pepper, red pepper, and oregano and placed on the dahneek to dry. It became black and mildewed, but it was stored this way (Informant 9).

Cheese was cut to the size of the palm of a hand. Informant 5 and Informant 46, from Amasia, said that it was then placed in an earthenware jar in layers alternating with layers of salt, with a salt layer on top. It was covered with a cabbage leaf, then closed so tightly that no air could enter. The jar was then partially buried upside-down in the earth. When cheese was needed, a jar was uprighted, the cheese removed as necessary, washed to remove the salt, and eaten. When that jar was empty, the next was uprighted. Sometimes the mouth of the jar was covered with cottage cheese in order to make it airtight before being buried (Informant 9). Others said that the mouth of the container was plastered with mud.

The Armenian village women also were responsible for preserving vegetables and fruits for winter use. In the month when produce was most plentiful, usually September, they started their work; Informant 19, from Sohngurlu, near Ankara, remarked that once harvest had begun, the ojakh often did not die down for a whole week as the women cooked for winter storage. Processing methods and the kinds of produce preserved obviously varied even more greatly than in the case of dairy products, but the following brief survey of some of them will suggest both the amount of labor and the time necessary to feed a typical household when little fresh food was available.

In the Amasia area, for example, the women hollowed tomatoes and dried them (Informant 46); in the Bursa area, they simply cut them in half before drying them (Informant 23). The dried fruits were then packed into petakner, and Informant 23 said that they became almost like fresh again when they were dropped into boiling water. Informant 37, from Akhalkalakh in Georgia, described a process in which whole tomatoes were carefully placed in jars and then covered with brine; she also knew of households in which the tomatoes were boiled into sauce, which was then stored in earthenware jars (according also to Informant 19). She knew of making tomato paste by squeezing out the tomato juice and boiling it until it thickened. Informant 12 said that such sauce was then poured into open pans and left in the sun to cook further; it was stored in jars filmed with oil.

Other procedures included such simple methods as threading certain green vegetables, legumes, and root crops on long strings and hanging them, either to dry in the sun or indoors, to be dried and stored simultaneously.

Several informants from different areas said that turnips, onions, potatoes, beets, and cabbages were often stored in a pit dug in the ground of the maran and covered with dirt to prevent freezing. Cabbage and mixed vegetable pickles, made in large quantities and stored in earthenware jars, were very popular. Such pickled foods served alone added variety to the winter diet, and they were also used in preparing other foods.

Nuts could be stored with little processing, and several fruits required little more than sun-drying. Sour cherries, apple slices, apricots, plums, and pears were strung and dried on the dahneek. Mulberries were dried to eat like raisins, made into rakhee, or cooked and placed in the sun. According to Informant 33, from Shabinkarahisar, near Sepastia, and Informant 12, green figs were slashed and dried, then quickly dropped into hot water, spread once again on a white sheet, and covered with another white sheet. The women stepped on the covered figs to flatten them. After drying a second time, the fruit was packed away.

As might be expected, however, grapes furnished a number of different products, each of which called for a particular kind of processing. Hung from the ceiling of a well-ventilated room, they could be kept to be eaten as fresh fruit, in some cases until as late as March (Informants 16, 17, 43, 48). Dried in the sun, they made raisins. Informant 15 described another process involving special large grapes. Ashes were dropped into a container of water; the next day the grapes were dipped into this water several times, then dipped into olive oil, and, finally, dried in the sun. In still another process, the grapes were put into a hot water bath, then set out to dry (Informant 12).

Bastegh was prepared by boiling grape juice (or the juice of some other fruit) with sugar or honey. When quite thick, it was spread out in thin layers over the surface of large white sheets and left in the sun to dry. When the drying was completed, the back of the sheet was slightly dampened and the bastegh was easily peeled away; it was cut into pieces and stored for winter treats. The tart juice of unprocessed grapes was also kept to be used in place of lemon.

If there were abundant vineyards in the area, villagers made wine. Informant 43, from Van, said that the young people stepped on the grapes and the juice poured into large containers placed to catch it. The juice fermented in these wooden or earthenware jars. If the top was closed too soon, however, the jar would burst. The wine was stored for at least three or four months before use.

The Armenian household used a number of things for cooking oil: butter, and less frequently, flax seed, olive, cottonseed, or sesame seed oils. Perhaps most popular was the oil obtained by rendering the fat available in a sheep's tail. In areas around Bursa, where olive trees grew by the sea, the olives were pitted and pressed with large rocks in order to extract the oil (Informant 23). In areas to the east, flax, which has a seed smaller than the sesame seed, was grown especially for its oil. The seeds were heated and crushed beneath large stone rollers. Four of these rollers were available in Van for the use of nearby villages (Informant 43). The flax seed oil, as well as sesame seed oil, was particularly important during Lent, when animal fat and butter could not be used; flax seed oil also had medicinal uses (Informant 29, from Chanakjee village, near Kughee).

In the fall, the men slaughtered the animals that they did not wish to maintain through the winter. Then they cooked any meat that was to be eaten fresh, either by roasting it or broiling it in small chunks on spits. (However, Informants 12, 13, and 41 all said that some Armenians saw fresh meat only at Easter and Christmas and at weddings and funerals). The women prepared *khavoorma* from the rest, cutting the lamb, or a combination of lamb and beef, into three- to four-inch cubes and boiling them until they were well-done and completely devoid of fat. Meanwhile, the women had chopped and cooked down the suet from the lamb's stomach. After the khavoorma had been packed into huge earthenware jars, the hot fat was poured over, filling any air pockets and completely sealing the surface. As the winter progressed, the women removed pieces of khavoorma from the petakner along with the rendered fat and used them together with vegetables and grains. Sometimes ground meat was stored in a similar way (Informant 46, from Amasia). However, according to Informant 41, even khavoorma was available only to moderately well off and wealthy families. Informant 17, from Kharadigin, near Erzunga, described the storage containers as being made of salty sand which was grainy to the touch.

Both Informant 5, from Kharzeet, and Informant 25, from Kughee, said that another way of preserving meat was to salt it heavily and weight it down with rocks. In some places beef was treated this way; in others both beef and lamb were used (Informant 4). In some areas, large pieces of meat were salted and dried in the sun (Informant 16, from Kharpert). When meat was needed, it was washed and soaked in water before it was cooked with beans, turnips, or cabbage. However, Informant 22, from Sepastia, said that in some areas the whole animal carcass was hung in the cold basement, and the women simply cut pieces as they needed them.

When fish was available, the women either salted and dried it, or pickled it in brine in petakner, which in this case were kept upright, rather than inverted as for other foods.

Household Routines

Normally, the Armenian village family ate three meals a day, although they might observe Wednesdays and Fridays as fast days, during which they ate no milk, meat, or fish. Evidently the Armenian diet, although wholesome enough to promote good health and longevity, frequently was frugal and monotonous. Cereals and dairy products dominate the memories of the Detroit informants. Beans—red, white, fava, lima—were also common to most; stews of various kinds were a staple. What follows is a general picture of the Armenian villager's daily meals, based on local details supplied by the entire group of informants. Naturally not all of the several items mentioned were prepared for the same meal, nor were they all necessarily characteristic of any one village or household.

Tea and bread in combination with some dairy product—milk, madzoon, cheese, or a prepared dish—was certainly the most usual breakfast fare; however, Informant 12, from Kessab, said that bread and syrup were common in her area. Various soups and stews, ordinarily with a madzoon or tahn base, were also popular. Cooked bulgher or other cereals, beans, honey, nuts, raisins, and olives were mentioned less frequently.

More often than not, lunch could be a repetition of breakfast, although the midday meal frequently provided items in addition to the usual bread, dairy products, and stews. Various kinds of pilaf, eggs, olives, beans, onions, and greens were likely; sometimes khavoorma was served. According to Informant 33, from Shabinkarahisar, schoolchildren took their lunches with them in copper bowls; at times they simply carried dried figs, raisins, and nuts in their pockets. Informant 21, from Meghoozeek, near Erzunga, said that only a few of the men who worked in the fields took their lunches with them. Normally the junior wife of the household carried trays to the fields and back.

Dinner was likely to include at least one dish prepared with some kind of cereal and one or more vegetables, sometimes also containing meat or fish. The meat usually was khavoorma, although in the larger villages, fresh meat was available from the butcher each week, or even several times a week (Informants 29, 21). Otherwise, dinner was very similar to breakfast and lunch.

Armenian village houses did not have the convenience of piped water nor of a municipal sewage system, so how an individual household managed the problems of safe drinking water, bathing, laundry, and disposal of human wastes depended to a large extent on its geographical location and the construction of its dwelling. Because the villages were located near natural water supplies, rivers, mountain streams, springs, or village wells, supplemented when necessary by collected rainwater or melted snow, provided enough water for ordinary daily use.

The women or young boys of the household had the primary responsibility for maintaining the domestic water supply. (Informant 5, from Kharzeet, said that men did not go to the village fountain.) Informant 12, from Kessab, where water was relatively scarce and there were no springs, said that the young village girls had to go up the mountain to fetch water from a brook. The task was particularly dangerous in the winter, when they had to descend the slippery rocks while burdened with heavy earthenware jugs or metal cans. In Efgere, the villagers used well water for drinking, laundry, and bathing water, but only after allowing their filled containers to stand for two days. The sand settled to the bottom, leaving clear water on top.

The Detroit informants did not offer much information about laundry facilities, probably because there were usually only two possibilities: those women who lived near rivers or where villages had a spring or well took their laundry there, or they washed in a tub in the household akhor or pag. The water frequently was heated in large kettles; in fact, Informant 37, from Akhalkalakh, and Informant 41, from Karakehoy, areas where the laundry was done away from home, mentioned that an ojakh had been built so that the village women could heat their water. The washerwoman trod the laundry with her bare feet—even in the winter, according to Informant 18—or pounded it with a club to remove the dirt. In the Kughee area, it was apparently common for women to sprinkle ashes in the water to get the clothes cleaner (Informants 25, 26).

Bathing required more privacy than laundry, and the group of informants named a variety of arrangements. In the summer, those who lived near rivers bathed there (Informant 17); others also might bathe outside, in an area of the pag away from the entrance. Often this was an enclosed space paved with stones, but a bather did not sit in a tub of water. Rather, she sat on another large stone while the household women poured water over her, using soap and a coarse canvas cloth, *keseh,* to cleanse and stimulate her skin.[11] In the winter, villagers bathed in the akhor or in the house itself. Tub bathing, in wooden tubs on stone-covered floors, or washing from copper basins, was necessary indoors (Informants 21, 24, 29, 36, 39), but the akhor arrangement allowed the poured water to run under the walls or through a hole in the floor (Informants 13, 24). Informant 5 remembered a paved area for washing and bathing located behind the cows—a very private place, because other family members entered only to feed or clean under the animals.

Although bathhouses were popular where they existed, they were to be found only in the larger and more prosperous villages.

Those who could went there once or twice a month, taking baths at home between visits. Informant 15, from Zeitoun, obviously recalled the bathhouse in her community with a great deal of pleasure. She remembered that a visit there involved much more than merely washing oneself. Families of women went together and spent most of the day, taking delicacies such as fruits, special *katah,* and nuts. The physical maturing of young girls into womanhood did not go unnoticed, and many a future mother-in-law quietly observed and compared young women, making possible choices for her young son. However, in time it came to pass that more girls than boys began to be born in this informant's town. The women believed that this was due to the hot baths, and some of them stopped using the bathhouse.

Toilet facilities ranged from simply a secluded spot in the garden or akhor through enclosed outhouses to ingenious arrangements that took advantage of nearby running water. Several informants from different areas described the toilet as high off the ground, completely enclosed, and located just inside the pag gate, far from the house (Informants 2, 10, 14, 16, 19, 22). In the spring, ashes were mixed with the accumulated feces and the mixture was used to fertilize the fields. The empty containers were washed down and replaced for another period of collection. Informant 33 spoke of hanging a piece of meat in a deep hole under the toilet hole. It was believed that the maggoty meat acted to disintegrate the feces. Informant 34, from Severeg, remembered a household toilet in a separate roofed building inside the pag; the space was tiled and inclined toward a little river. By the simple expedient of pouring water down the toilet hole every few days, the waste matter was moved directly into the running water.

Clothing

The traditional dress of the Armenians was similar to that of their neighbors and well adapted to their way of life. Small children of both sexes were dressed in long shifts. Men and some women wore baggy trousers that reached the ankle, a matter of convenience, especially in cold weather, to people who often sat on the floor. Both sexes also covered their heads, thereby providing insulation against both heat and cold. Wool was the most common fiber used, but many could afford to buy cotton, linen, or silk cloth for undergarments and summer wear.

In Eastern Armenia affluent men dressed like other Caucasian mountaineers, wearing a shirt with a low collar, buttoned from the side, baggy pants, an *arkhalugh* (a belted coat buttoned with small buttons from collar to knees), a dark overcoat reaching the ankles, a sheepskin cap, and artisan-made boots or slippers. In the villages the men wrapped their baggy pants with wide puttees attached to the edge of knitted socks, and wore homemade leather footwear. In winter they used sheepskin coats. In Western Armenia, the men wore a sleeveless vest and a short, waist-length jacket along with their shirts and baggy pants. Around the waist they wore a colored sash. Their hats were often semispherical and wrapped with a scarf.[12]

According to Lisitsian, women in Eastern Armenia preferred the color red, believing that it warded off evil. As undergarments they wore a shift and baggy pants. Like the men, they wore an arkhalugh, but it reached down almost to their heels. In winter rich women wore a red velvet overcoat edged with fur. Married women wore a "tower" headdress in the presence of men. They covered their hair and the lower part of their faces up to the nose. On the tower headdress were gold and silver coins and coral pendants. The women also wore rings, but no bracelets or necklaces.

In Western Armenia women also wore a shift and baggy pants, together with an overdress and an apron from the waist down. While married women kept their hair covered with scarves, in most places they did not cover the lower part of their faces. Girls liked to braid their hair in many braids, plaiting in threads and tying it with ribbons. Western Armenian women loved jewelry, and wore necklaces and bracelets on both arms and legs. In general, there was more embroidery on the clothing of Western Armenians than on that of their eastern kinsmen.

The "luxury" aspects of Armenian dress represented an investment for affluent families. Since there were no banks, the Armenian woman walked around with much of the family savings on her person. A nineteenth-century observer remarked that in any case, "what a woman wears on her person, no one can take for her husband's debts."[13] Even today, Armenians in Soviet Armenia distrust paper currency and prefer to invest in gold and silver jewelry.

Comparisons

The housing, diet, and dress of the Armenians at the turn of the century represented intelligent strategies of energy conservation. Under normal conditions, their simple economy provided subsistence goods and the means to pay rents and taxes. Since there were no large urban markets in Armenia, they could not have profited from specialized commercial farming. Some of the sanitary practices of the Armenians likewise were excellent: they used spring water, boiled raw milk, and took steam baths regularly. Since most were ignorant of the germ theory of disease and lacked adequate sewage systems, however, their mortality rate from contagious diseases was high.

In sum, despite the ingenuity of its people, Armenia was not well suited to food production and could not support a dense population at the turn of the century. Arable land constituted only one-third of the total, the growing season was short, and there was so little wood that animal dung had to be used for fuel instead of fertilizer. The natural economic assets of Armenia were chiefly minerals, but these could not be fully utilized until the area was industrialized.

Many traits of Armenian material culture were similar to those of neighboring peoples. There was a widespread tendency to rural self-sufficiency throughout the Eastern Mediterranean lands, Iran, and Anatolia, for very few areas were served by navigable rivers, and land transport was expensive. Since there were few large cities, most peasants had only a limited market for surplus products, and most commerce tended to be local and small-scale. Consequently, people lived in small, isolated, but rather similar worlds.

Communities commonly engaged in both agriculture and animal husbandry. In lands where mountains provided summer pasture, and valleys gave winter shelter and arable soil, peasants commonly divided their energies between the two areas. This pattern of transhumance was found among Greeks, Kurds, and Turks as well as Armenians. In such areas a diet of cereals, dairy products, fruits, and vegetables was typical; peasants ate little meat. Similar forms of flat bread, and reverential attitudes toward bread, have been found among many peoples around the Mediterranean Sea.[14]

Where wood was scarce—in Central Anatolia, Iran, Syria, and much of Greece—the people burned dried dung for fuel. They constructed their homes mainly of mud brick and stone, using wood only for pillars, doors, reinforcements, and roofs, and there was very little wooden furniture in the Armenian home. In the colder parts of Anatolia and Transcaucasia, peasants conserved heat by crowding into a single windowless room around a sunken fireplace in winter.[15] Similarly, in early modern England and France, where wood was also scarce and expensive, the peasant family usually slept in the cow stable in winter, or sometimes in a single bed.[16]

Since prehistoric times men were usually the ones who cared for the larger domestic animals, and this tradition had a number of interesting influences on customs. Among the Turks and Hungarians as well as the Armenians, it was customary for the men to have a special clubroom in the stable for winter socializing. This was also a place where they entertained outside visitors.[17] Another widespread custom was for men, on festive occasions, to take charge of roasting fresh meat out of doors. The division of village space into "men's space" and "women's space" was widespread in eastern Europe and also noted in southern France.[18]

An Armenian woman is making butter in an earthenware churn, using a rocking motion.

A group of Armenian neighbors baking bread in the village of Van.

Young Armenians in their native dress at a family dinner in Van.

Children weaving rugs in an Armenian-American orphanage.

Armenian villagers on the threshing floor (where grain is separated from wheat) in village of Van.

Bridal gowns worn in Sepastia.

Armenian villagers gathering for a wedding.

Pilgrims in a sacred place near Dharma Village.

Celebration at the sacred place of St. Charles in Moosh Sultan.

An Armenian monastery.

Monastery of St. Neshan.

View of the village of Zeitoun.

Turkish post office.

View of the city of Adana.

3.

BETROTHAL AND MARRIAGE

It was the Armenian woman who made the existence of the extended family household possible. The drying and storage of fruits and vegetables; the preservation of dairy products; the preparation of pickled vegetables; the grinding, sorting, and storage of various grains; the baking of mountains of lavash; and the creation of new combinations of grains, dairy products, and vegetables to satisfy the hungry appetites day after day was a Herculean task. Yet her very importance at the center of the household meant that her horizons in the larger world were very limited. From the moment of her birth, the typical Armenian village girl lived and died within a male-dominated society. When, in describing the ceremonies of a village wedding, Informant 9 repeatedly referred to the groom as "the king," she revealed even more than she intended about the culture of her youth.

Whether a village girl received a formal education depended on the availability of a school and the progressiveness of her family. If a particular village had a school, both boys and girls of elementary school age might attend, but if it were necessary to walk to a neighboring village for classes, only the boys were allowed to go. In some cases, if a girl's father or other male relatives believed that an education would corrupt her, she was purposely kept illiterate. Susie Hoogasian Villa's grandmother, who was born and raised in a town, was kept illiterate because her four brothers feared that she would write love letters if she learned to read and write. The family's religious affiliation was another important influence on determining whether a girl went to school. One of the greatest contributions of the

American missionaries was that their educational system was open
to both sexes, whereas the Armenian parochial school was limited,
for the most part, to males. Moreover, girls who attended Protestant schools tended to marry later than other village girls, a very
important consideration in terms of personal development.

Yet there is no doubt that the marriage ceremony was the single
most decisive event in the life of the Armenian village woman. In
most areas, the maiden had considerable freedom of movement
before marriage.[1] Once she had participated in this rite of passage,
however, she became mute, lost her individuality, and fell under
the absolute control of her elders. It is true that there was some
recompense: if this mute bride lived long enough to become the
matriarch of the gerdastan, she ruled supreme over sons and
daughters-in-law, treated with the greatest respect and enjoying
many privileges.

Betrothal

The Armenian wedding was a profoundly important social event,
an alliance not just between individuals, but also between groups.
As the family saw it, the bride would be not just the groom's bride,
but their bride. All members of the bride's and groom's families
became in-laws (*khnamee*). A marriage, therefore, sent ripples
through clans and communities, and engagements could not be
undertaken lightly. Indeed, the prospective bride and groom often
had little to say in the matter.

It was necessary to examine certain matters before seriously
considering any betrothal. According to church law, the two princi-
pals must be separated by seven "navels".[2] In other words, marriage could not rightfully occur if there was a blood relationship
closer than seven steps; therefore, the lineage of each of the prospective partners had to be studied and compared. Furthermore,
the leaders of the Armenian wedding were the *kavor* and the *kavorgeen* of the groom. These were either the godparents of the
groom himself or would be the godparents of his future children.

Marriage between members of families in this relationship was forbidden, up to and including second cousins.

Ordinarily girls were married young, and it was not uncommon for prepubescent girls to be married in order to protect them from the Turks, who preferred virgins to married women. Generally speaking, the more physically or politically insecure the villagers felt, the younger the age for marriage. Informant 46, from Amasia, for example, said that while her grandmother had been married at eleven, her mother did not marry until sixteen. Girls of fourteen, fifteen, sixteen, and seventeen were married in Van and Bursa; some said that girls of nineteen or twenty were considered to be *doon-mnah* ("left at home" or old maids) and only good enough to marry widowers with children and be taken away to another village. Boys usually were engaged when they were between fifteen and twenty years old.[3]

The choice of a prospective bride could occur in several different ways and might involve third parties from outside the family. Sometimes two male friends decided to marry their son and daughter to each other when they came of age. This early promising frequently occurred when the girl was still in her cradle; it was often sealed by payment of a coin. The families waited until the girl's first menstruation to celebrate the engagement. Sometimes a helpful relative of the boy started the procedure. Perhaps he had stopped for the night at the girl's home in his travels from one place to another. Reports on a family's reputation, as well as on the industry and modest character of the young daughter, were especially easy to ascertain in the village of an in-law family. Sometimes the boy's family hired a *meechnordt* ("go-between" or matchmaker), an old woman who, because of her many social contacts, could find a suitable wife; perhaps a man with several marriageable daughters might ask such a woman to direct interested suitors to his household. (As a rule, the oldest girl had to marry first, and a younger sister's engagement could last for years if her wedding had to wait upon her elder's.) According to Informant 39, from Hajin, it was even possible for a boy's family to take a young girl whose mother had died into their own household and raise her to the age when she could be married to their son.

The future bride and groom might or might not know each other before they were betrothed, but there were opportunities for young people to meet in the course of daily living, and there is certainly evidence to suggest that a boy (or even a girl) could sometimes influence his family to choose the one he preferred. In small communities, it was almost inevitable that the betrothed pair would have some earlier acquaintance. Informant 3, from Karaghil, declared that it was entirely possible for a boy to notice a girl and indicate his choice to his parents. It was their responsibility to inquire about her and her family's reputations. Informant 41, from Karakehoy, also said that the boy had some say in the choice of his future bride.

Informant 47, who practiced folk healing and fortune-telling, said that young people of either sex who had fallen in love might resort to magic to gain their beloved's favor—though none of the ways she mentioned seems to have solved the problem of what to do if the families objected.

> When a boy is eager to marry a girl who does not reciprocate his feelings, he takes a strand of his hair to the Turkish fortune-teller [probably a dervish] who, with his power and knowledge of magic, makes three pieces of paper from it.
>
> The boy places one of these in the doorway of the girl's house so that every time she enters or leaves, she will pass over it. The second, he buries in her oven so that everything which she eats will have had contact with it. The third, he manages to have her drink [pulverized, perhaps]. When he succeeds in doing all three of these things, it is believed that the girl will love and be eager to marry.

> If a girl mixes her menstrual blood (or hair burned to ashes, or nails filed to a powder) with a beverage and gives it to a young man, she will cause him to fall in love with her and be eager for marriage.

However, Informant 9, from Govdun, maintained that young people would elope if they loved one another and were not allowed to marry.[4]

The two families typically carried out protracted and somewhat ritualistic negotiations before the formal engagement. Depending on the particular situation, a relative, in-law, or hired female matchmaker might begin the process by first contacting the mother of the bride. If she were interested, some male members of the boy's family, usually led by a paternal uncle, would come to negotiate, subtly and indirectly, with the girl's family. Neither the boy nor girl were present, of course, and by leaving out the boy's father as well, the groom's family could avoid being embarrassed if the negotiations failed.

During negotiations the girl's family served coffee to the representatives of the boy's family. According to some Detroit informants, if the coffee were bitter, that was a way of saying no. The parents of the girl would usually procrastinate by saying, "We must ask her godfather. We must ask her mother's brother. We must ask her father's brother," and so on. Often, after the arrangements were pretty much complete, the girl was told about the proposal. "Do you accept this?" she was sometimes asked. The girl looked down at her feet and, deferring to the judgment of her elders, replied as she was expected to do: "You know about these things" (Informant 1, from Erzunga). Meanwhile, both sides investigated the physical, mental, and emotional attributes of both candidates. The women from the boy's family would try to look over the girl in the public bathhouse to see if she had any physical defects. In addition, the two families would bargain over how much each was to contribute to the girl's dowry and the expenses of the wedding.

Usually the boy's family ascertained in advance that their proposal would be accepted before they formally made it. When they did so, the girl's father might first consult, or present the views of, each member of the family, moving from the least to the most important, before giving his own consent. With the acceptance of the girl's father, "the word was tied" (*khosk kap*). The boy's representatives went home and told him, "We have received their word" (*khosk arenk*). Then the female members of the two families began to exchange visits.

The girl's family's first visit to the boy's home was called *pesah des;* this event initiated *khnamoutiun* ("in-law relationship"), which lasted for a period of a few months to two or more years. During such visiting back and forth between the two families, the young boy and girl were not permitted to talk to each other. Even after the formal engagement, the boy saw the girl only with her family. Sometimes, by conniving with neighbors, he could manage to see her alone at their house (Informant 41).

The formal betrothal was usually a party at the girl's home, at which the boy and girl might or might not be present. Most Detroit informants indicated that they were. The boy's family presented the girl's with a ring or other ornament called a "sign" (*nshan*). There was food, drink, music, and dancing, sometimes lasting for two days. The priest brought the couple before him and had them touch their foreheads together while they held lighted candles. The girl's face was covered with a veil. The boy's mother put the ring or other jewelry on the girl. The boy's godfather held a cross at the end of a long wooden pole over the heads of the couple throughout the ceremony, and the priest instructed them in the joys and responsibilities of Armenian marriage and family. Informant 7, from Efgere, said that the guests gave gifts of money to the bride at the end of this ceremony. Informant 21, from Meghoozeek, remembered that the priest's wife asked for a screen, flour, and a knife. She sifted the flour through the screen and then cut it with the knife to signify that a girl is like a knife: she has no tongue until it is opened in the house of her husband. These villagers also put a red necktie on the groom-to-be, which signified the hymenal blood. Informant 15, however, averred that people in Zeitoun were serious—they did not have a party.

Informant 10, from Caesarea, Informant 22, from Sepastia, and Informant 23, from Chengiler, near Bursa, said that a bracelet or gold coins were usually given as the nshan instead of a ring. Particularly in the small villages, however, families might have neither jewelry nor money to give, and in those cases some other item— perhaps something belonging to the boy's mother (Informant 13, from Akor village)—served the same purpose. According to Informant 7, occasionally the girl's family gave the boy a ring.

Some particulars showing variations in the courtship and engagement pattern are interesting and worth noting. For example, Informant 26, from Hakusdun, remembered that neither she nor her future husband had anything to say about the marriage choice. For the engagement, a ring was brought to her house and left there.

She was not even home at the time. In Shabinkarahisar, once the betrothal was arranged, the priest blessed the nshan at the boy's house and the boy's family took it to the girl; the boy did not accompany them (Informant 33). Informant 29, from Chanakjee village, said that in some villages the boy's godmother was responsible for preparing large kettles of *helva,* a sweet farina pudding. Informant 48, from Harseg village, near Kharpert, said that in her area helva and bread were sent to neighbors, friends, and relatives, near and far, as an invitation to attend the engagement ceremonies. According to Informant 46, from Amasia, the kavor and kavorgeen, the groom-to-be, his mother and father, and their priest journeyed to the girl's house with the nshan and a tray of confections, usually almonds wrapped in netting. In Severeg, according to Informant 34, the men of both families met in the church with no women present. An attractive tray of sweets was arranged around the nshan. The priest blessed this; the men ate the confections. Then the girl's father returned to his home with the empty tray.

We are fortunate in having an especially full description of betrothal customs and attitudes toward the prospective bride in the Kessab area (Informant 12). There the boy's father arranged the engagement party; the girl's family had no part in it. He, the boy, and other relatives took the nshan to the girl, and frequently this was the first time she saw her betrothed. Every one of the boy's female relatives prepared sweets, and there might be as many as forty trays of them. Indeed, it might be said of an attractive girl that when she married, "This girl will go for forty or fifty *seenee(s)* (baking trays)." Carrying the trays on their heads, the women sang or called, "Lu, lu, lu." Thus they went to the girl's house. Meanwhile, her father, having been told of this visit, had asked his relatives to come to his house.

The father served coffee and other drinks. The girl kissed the hands of each woman present, from the oldest to the youngest. They put a coin in her hands; she slipped it into a handkerchief. They pressed her to talk, but she would not. The more full-bodied the girl, the more they liked her. "By God! This is a woman!" they said about a hefty maiden. Meanwhile, each person who knew the girl's family came for *achkee looysee* ("congratulations") and was served some of the pastry. Then the boy and his friends came to the girl's house and were treated to an omelette served with syrup.

There was a ceremony when the boy presented the ring, which was used for both the engagement and the wedding. The girl wore it on her right hand until the wedding, when it was transferred to her left. Another ceremony took place when the bride's clothes and wedding clothing for her own womenfolk were prepared. The boy's family usually presented the cloth on the Thursday of the wedding week; the gowns had to be sewn by Saturday, because the wedding would be on Sunday.

Wedding

The ceremonies surrounding the Armenian wedding were protracted and elaborate. As the Detroit informants recalled the practices in their native communities, they frequently supplied clues to communal attitudes that they might not have been able to describe if asked about them directly. I have therefore chosen to base the general description of the wedding customs on the testimony of informants from the Kharpert area[5]—Susie Hoogasian Villa's parents' native region—providing specific details for other localities when they reveal a particularly interesting variation. The broad outlines of the activities remain the same throughout Armenia.

Ordinarily the wedding took place within a year after the formal betrothal, although it was possible that several years might pass. However, a family could not break an engagement without paying the other family compensation for loss of face.

A wedding reception (*harsaneek*) might last one to seven days, the average being three days. Typically, the ritual began on Friday, the church service was held on Saturday, and consummation occurred on Sunday night. The favored times of the year were fall, before the pre-Christmas fast, and winter, before the beginning of Lent; no engagements or weddings were allowed during the Lenten period. (Informant 3, from Karaghil, and Informant 14, from Gavra village, said that a spring wedding was called a *dzour bsag* ["crooked wedding" or wedding at unacceptable time of year].) At these times the heaviest labor of the year was over. In fall people were killing surplus animals that they did not wish to support over the winter, so that sacrifice of an animal for the wedding feast was not such a great loss, and food was generally abundant. By January, on the other hand, the wine from the grape harvest of the preceding summer was ready to drink.

Both the groom and the bride underwent special preparation before the wedding. One of the most interesting differences between their experiences is that generally the young man was readied for the day with much laughter and horseplay, while the girl and her family spent much of their remaining time together lamenting.

Several days before the wedding, the women of the boy's household took a large dish of henna, handsomely decorated with fruits and nuts, to the girl. Friends and neighbors—usually women—gathered at the girl's house to dye her fingers and toes lightly with the henna (Informant 48) (Turkish custom adopted by some Armenians to insure fertility). When the dye had set and was ready to be removed, the girl's womenfolk, or sometimes the groom's, took the girl to the bathhouse or gave her a bath in the pag or in the cooking area. After the bath, they joined the larger group and produced the wedding garments which they had brought with them, and which the bride may not have seen until that moment.

According to Informant 5, from Kharzeet, while attending the bride the women sometimes sang,

> *Or, or*
> From seven stores, I gathered silver and made a ring,
> And put it on Pearl's finger.

Informants 31 and 32 recalled that a bride reluctant to marry a man not of her choice sang these words with her mother:

Mother: Bride, don't cry, don't cry, your eyes will hurt. May he who married you so young, may his household topple.

Girl: Why should I not cry, Mother? You [plural] fooled me. You didn't give me to the one I loved; you have made my heart yearn.

Mother: He is young and poor; he has no house, no position, nothing.

Girl: His condition is good; what should I do with a house? If it were only a nest, if you had given me to my loved one, I would have been satisfied with my loved one.

The bride-to-be was dressed by her friends or her own godmother, but the veil was sometimes put in place by the kavorgeen. The bride's wedding dress was usually provided by her parents. One bride in Shabinkarahisar wore an overcoat with three panels and a weskit jacket made of velvet embroidered with gold thread. A round, dishlike ornament, sometimes decorated with pearls, rested high on the bride's head and a chain of gold decorations was worn across her forehead. The veil was usually red. (In the last few years before the war, however, more modern dress was worn.) In Van, as in most places, the bridal dress did not have to be a specific color, but it was usually silk taffeta or cotton. Informant 5 recalled a bride in a red taffeta dress and blue velvet apron embroidered with shiny threads. Sometimes the bride fashioned a kerchief trimmed with coins that would tie under her chin and frame her face. The bride also wore a red *yazma,* a kind of veil, over another veil of white silk. This inner veil was not removed at the church, and not until the marriage was consummated did the groom see his wife. Even after the wedding, she remained veiled in public until her first child was born.

The kavor, accompanied by the boy's friends, took him to be shaved and bathed. This occurred at a public bathhouse if there were one accessible; otherwise they used the bathing area in the stable. Most Armenian villages did not have a local resident skilled in barbering, and instead relied on the services of an itinerant barber who visited the villages once a week. This man was usually paid in the fall when the harvest brought a few coins to the village families. It was the kavor's responsibility to bring the barber to the village and to supervise his work, while the other village youths gathered around shouting encouragement. The barber, who had been looking forward to this opportunity, suddenly exclaimed in song and verse. Only when the kavor paid him a bonus did the work continue.

On the day of the wedding, the girl's own parish priest arrived at the house to bless the wedding garments before they were worn. Very often, a *ges bsag* ("half-wedding") occurred at the girl's house, a ceremony which was supposed to make it impossible for the girl's parents to substitute an ugly daughter for the promised bride. Furthermore, if the girl's parents did not attend the church ceremony, this was the only religious observation they shared. The bride's own godmother (some say the groom's godmother) then began to dress the girl in preparation for her final leave-taking from the house of her childhood. Informant 38 recalled one mother's advice to her daughter, the bride.

Mother: Be a happy neighbor; with your head and your mind be alert.
Be worthy of your father-in-law and your mother-in-law;
Live as you have seen your father and mother live.

Girl: I will never forget my native mother, Armenia.

Informant 1, from Erzunga, remembered hearing one bride sing this song with her godmother:

Bride: Let me kiss your hand, Mother,
I have eaten your sweet milk.

Godmother: Have intelligence, grace, and love.
Go, my child. God will be with you.

Sometimes the bridal attendants sang; at other times a skilled village balladeer was brought in for this occasion. More often, the bride herself sang laments to her parents. Informant 2, from Fenesé, near Caesarea, recited Armenian versions of two Turkish songs that the bride might sing in order to make her mother cry. The first one originally may have been a dialogue between the girl and her mother.

The girl's mother is now without her daughter. My place is now a wilderness. I will be free from your hands and go away. I left and went away; my place is empty. Your flower remains dry. I will not come to your side again.

I drank your milk when I was small. Break my spoon and throw it in the garden. Give my portion of food to the poor.

Another song of parting began, "Come, father, you have fed her, kiss her now before she leaves you." The father entered and hugged his daughter, while everywhere there was sadness and loud wailing. In the Kughee area, according to Informant 26, from Hakusdun, two men in the bride's family usually sang

> *Sharum, shar-sharum, sharum, shar-sharum.*
> They have come to take me; they have come to take me.
> Let them take you; let them take you.
> We will bring you back at Easter.
> Tie the *garbuj* [?]; place it on the bride.
> Take her to the garden; pick apples;
> Arrange them in a belt and place it on the bride.
> *Sharum, shar-sharum,* tomorrow I will leave.
> Let them take you; they will bring you back at Easter.
> Ah apple, chief apple, you will see one day,
> Ah apple, chief apple, you will see one day,
> [meaning obscure].

They wore belts of large cakes to give them the strength to sing such mournful things. A common saying was, "The household sat on the wood," referring to the wooden slats sometimes placed on the toneer when the fire had burnt out and the embers were smoldering.

Meanwhile the groom's happy procession, accompanied by drum and horn, had reached the girl's house to claim the bride. If the bride-to-be lived in the groom's own village, his family often called for her by walking to her house. However, if she lived outside the village, they came to claim her in a procession with at least one horse. Often the groom's family and relatives formed the group, while he waited patiently at the church. As they attempted to enter the bride's house, they often found the door locked. Only when the kavor rewarded the future brother-in-law with a coin did the procession move inside. If the groom had accompanied the group, he kissed the hand of his future mother-in-law, who then usually gave him a small gift which she had made for him. In villages where locking the door of the bridal house did not occur, the bride's brother claimed a boon in a different manner. He quickly mounted whichever horse the bride was destined to ride and did not come down until the groom or his godfather slipped him a coin.

With song and rejoicing, the wedding procession went directly to the church in the groom's parish or village. If the boy's village were far away, the girl spent the night at the kavor's house. The girl's parents rarely joined this group: their daughter had left the house and they had no further claim on her. However, other members of the family, such as brothers, sisters, aunts, and uncles, did not often stay behind.

At the church, the marriage ceremony was performed with the young people brought forehead to forehead, nose to nose, hand to hand. The bride's face was covered with a half-veil; both bride and groom held lighted candles, and the godfather again held the cross high above their heads. Blessed ribbons or threads (crowns, in earlier times) called the *narod* were tied around the forehead of each. At one time, the narod was worn three to eight days, during which time the marriage could not be consummated. However, many of the informants indicated that the priest visited the wedding feast and untied the ribbons. Other informants indicated that the narod was removed even before the young people left the church. Informant 25, from Kughee, remembered hearing that if the bride stepped on the groom's foot during the ceremony, she would have the upper hand in the marriage.

At the close of the ceremony, the bride was led to her new home by her husband, resplendent with a sword at his side. Some said that because of the many complaints made to the government about the Kurds who, fully armed, galloped out of nowhere and snatched away the new bride, the Turkish government had given the groom the right to carry a sword on his marriage day.

Relatives and neighbors each had prepared tables of appetizers in front of their houses. As the party passed these residences, they ate and drank, prolonging the return to the groom's house by hours. As he came closer to the family home, however, the bridegroom was in danger of being kidnapped by his playful attendants. If this happened, the groom could not return to the wedding festivities until the kavor paid a price which the pranksters used for their own fun later.

Upon the arrival of the newlyweds at the family household, the bridegroom slit the throat of a lamb, or, if he were poor, a rooster; this *madagh* ("offering," "sacrifice") was meant to prevent the entrance of illness and evil spirits. The couple stepped on the blood as they entered the house. In the Bursa area, according to Informant 23, the newlyweds' foreheads were also marked with blood. Informant 4, however, said that there was no such sacrifice in the Moush area. Instead, two or three lavash were placed on the bride's head and she walked to all corners of her husband's home before removing them. In most villages, the mother-in-law, singing "you are welcome, you are welcome," placed an earthenware plate, a jug of water, or a jar of candies in the hands of the new bride, instructing her to shatter it against the threshold, and often, in order to show his strength, the bridegroom was required to throw an apple at the door with such force that the apple would break into pieces.[6] Informant 41 reported that in the Adana area the door was opened from the inside as the bride threw a pomegranate to symbolize that her good luck had entered the house. In the Van region, the bride was made to step on eggs before entering (Informant 5). In the village of Shabinkarahisar, once the groom had entered, his family stole his shoe, and a reward had to be paid to regain it.

In the house there was food and merriment for all assembled.[7] Informant 43, from Van, said that an *asa bash*, a kind of master of ceremonies, chosen by the groom's friends from among themselves the night before the wedding, presided at the open house, but none of the other Detroit informants mentioned this feature. The veiled bride was led to a corner and left standing there as a spectator;[8] according to Informant 5, she was seated in a corner behind a drawn curtain, attended only by her bridesmaid. A supply of dried fruits, nuts, and candies was in readiness in a drawstring bag attached to a belt at her waist or wrist for the numerous requests of relatives and guests who approached her asking for *daross* ("similar fortune," the appropriate phrase for any occasion when congratulations are offered). She was obliged to reward them with a fistful of sweets, remaining silent and never casting her eyes to their faces. She kissed the hands of all guests who approached, young and old, male as well as female. Sometimes the kavorgeen held a dish in which she collected coins from the guests whom the bride kissed. The informants from Shabinkarahisar remembered that children were told that their hands would become white with the kiss.

When the festivities finally were over, it was time to take the newly wedded couple to the marriage bed. If the house had a second story, the bed was prepared there; otherwise, it was placed in the maran or perhaps in a room overlooking the akhor. However, in some villages, the attendants of the bride and groom remained nearby when the couple retired, the girls trying to snatch away some article of clothing belonging to the groom, while the men attempted to do the same with the bride's garments. Needless to say, under even the best circumstances, privacy was difficult or impossible to achieve.

All Detroit informants agreed that in town as well as village, for rich and poor alike, the virginity of the bride was essential. Proof of virginity, usually presented as a bloody sheet from the marriage bed, satisfied the groom's family and brought *badeev* ("honor") to the girl's. As Informant 22, from Sepastia put it, the sheet was sent or taken to the girl's mother to say achkee looys, with appreciation that she had raised a good girl and that her forehead was "open," not clouded. Informant 22 also said that either the groom or the groom's mother gave the bride a small gift following the proof, and on the Saturday after the wedding, the women took the bride to the bathhouse and enjoyed a party there. According to Informant 26, from Hakusdun, the boy's mother sent a red apple in a red handkerchief to the girl's parents as a sign of the bride's virginity.

Most informants, when asked what would have happened if the

bride were not a virgin, indicated that they did not know because the situation had never occurred. Nevertheless, they thought that in such a case she certainly would have been sent back home. Perhaps under some unusual circumstances, they said, the boy's family could decide to keep such a wife, but none had heard of this happening. Informant 24, from Aralez, near Van, said that if any woman were unchaste she would be beaten and her face muddied; she would then be put on a horse and sent out of the village—"to Russia or someplace." Informant 15, from Zeitoun, did remember a case when the daughter of a rich man had become pregnant out of wedlock. The townspeople smeared mud on her face, put her on a donkey with her child in her arms, and made her parade through every street. No one would marry her after that, and her child was not considered a human being.

Divorce did not occur among Armenians in the countryside. In case of adultery (an almost unheard-of offense), the villagers would cut the hair of the offending female, seat her backwards on a donkey, and parade her through the village to the sound of horn and drum. A man might be punished in the same way.[9]

With the wedding ceremony over and the bride's honor established, the newly united families began a period of consolidating the in-law relationship. Fifteen days after the wedding (ordinarily; other times, including the wedding day itself, were possible), the girl's parents came to visit her, bringing her trousseau with them. In anticipation of her marriage, the bride and her family had prepared a chest for her over many years. This contained outstanding examples of her own handwork, both with the needle and on the loom, as well as clothing enough to last her for a long time. Sometimes the trousseau was limited to these items; in other cases the bride had prepared many gifts, such as stockings, scarves, handkerchiefs, gloves, woolen leg wrappings, embroidered aprons for the women, and embroidered white pants for the men. Well-to-do town families undoubtedly included the bridal linens and plateware for the household, but this was seldom if ever done among the village peasantry. The girl's family might give her a cow or horse instead.

There was a small celebration and excitement over the trousseau as everyone examined the items. The girl's parents then returned to their home, and, as a rule, did not see their daughter again until she was sent home for a brief stay, either just before the delivery of her first child or after the first major holiday, usually Easter. Informant 18, from Khorsana village, near Sepastia, and Informant 25, from Kughee, said that the new wife did not have to wait until Easter. She could visit her maternal home after forty days, but she needed her mother-in-law's consent. Some recently married women spent a few days at Christmas with their parents, but this was exceptional. (In the towns, the boy's family usually was more liberal about permitting their *hars*, "daughter-in-law," to visit her parents.)

The songs of lament sung when the bride was being dressed for the wedding said that although she was leaving her maternal home, she would return at Easter. This visit was known as *marantz yertal* ("visit to mother"). According to Informant 32, from Shabinkara-hisar, the new wife returned from marantz yertal with a great number of red hard-boiled eggs, the traditional Armenian Easter eggs, for her husband's family. Khanamee(s) also usually exchanged gifts of pastries at Easter. Longer visits, of two weeks to a month, were possible after the wife had been in her husband's home for a while, according to Informant 4, from Vardo-Gunde-mir. When it was time for her to return, her husband's family came to fetch her, carrying food and delicacies for her family.

Widowhood and Remarriage

Because divorce was unknown, only widows or widowers were concerned with second marriages. In the towns, it was possible for a widow to support herself without remarrying by going from house to house, baking large quantities of bread in exchange for a few pieces to take home. Others could do laundry, sew, make lace, or weave cloth in exchange for food. Some widows worked as midwives or as nannies for rich children. If a widow worked as a servant in a wealthy home, she was usually permitted to keep her own children with her.

In the villages, however, the widow's fortunes depended more on the circumstances of the individual household of which she was a part. If a husband in a large gerdastan died, the widow and her children could remain in the household with little change in their lives. If the widow decided to remarry, the husband's family frequently insisted that she leave her children with them, although she had a better chance of taking them with her if the husband's family were poor. Informant 39, from Hajin, however, remarked that the first husband's family never forgot his widow—love was twofold for her. This informant said that the widow was usually encouraged to remarry, and, in fact, if the family had an unmarried son, they tried to marry her to him.

In speaking of remarriage, Informant 5 described what he clearly saw as an unusual arrangement. When a particular widow remarried, her late husband's share of his family's property was transferred to her sons. Her new husband tended to these lands until her sons came of age, at which time the boys left their stepfather's household and returned to their paternal home. Thus, although the sons had been with their mother in her second marriage, they returned to take their rightful places in their natural father's gerdastan. This informant also said that women who had property but no menfolk to care for it could call upon their neighbors, who would help out and divide the harvest accordingly.

Comparisons

Many parallels may be found between the Armenian wedding ritual and those of other peoples of eastern Europe and the Near East, for in this area the extended family household was the ideal. One function of the wedding ritual everywhere was to facilitate the transfer of the bride from one household to another. This meant that she must transfer her loyalty from one hearth to another. The Eastern Slavs and Georgians also considered it abnormal for the husband to live with his wife's family. Their women could also dispose of their capital as they wished after marriage.

At the same time, the wedding ritual celebrated one's coming of age. The bride began to cover her hair, as did all adult married women. The groom established his potency. While both were still junior members of a household, they had made an important step toward full adult status. Finally, the wedding ritual was intended to promote conception and successful childbearing. It contained sexual symbols and magic devices to protect the bride and groom from evil spirits.

Many Armenian wedding customs were widespread in eastern Europe as well: the giving of a ring, the veiling of the bride, the throwing of seed and fruits upon her to make her fertile, and the obstruction of the groom's party by her relatives.[10] The "half-wedding" at the bride's house was also found among the Georgians, but the Georgian groom was not present.[11] The public demonstration of the bloodied wedding bed sheet or of the bride's shift as proof of her virginity at marriage was especially widespread in the Mediterranean, eastern Europe, and the Near East at the turn of the century: it was found among Sicilians, Turks, Arabs, Kurds, the Eastern and Southern Slavs, Macedonians, Greeks, and Persians. It still prevails in many part of the Near East today.[12]

Punishing individuals who broke the sexual and marital rules of the community by making them ride backwards on a donkey was a common custom in early modern Europe.

The role of godparents, and the institution of god-kinship, was also widespread. It could be found among the Spaniards, Italians, Greeks, Serbs, Albanians, Ukrainians, and Hungarians. God-kin provided each other with economic and sometimes political assistance.[13] A similar institution called *kirvilik*, sponsorship at a circumcision ritual, was found among Turks, Kurds, Northern Iranians, Arabs in northern Iraq, and other Muslims in Western Armenia and Transcaucasia.[14]

When one turns from wedding rituals to marriage rules, one finds some important differences between Muslims and Christians. Islamic law permitted polygyny; Christian law did not. Islamic law permitted a man to divorce his wife; Christian law did so under rare circumstances, and in rural areas this almost never occurred. Islamic law allowed second and even first cousins to marry; Christian law forbade this without dispensation from the head of the church. Finally, the Muslim husband might sometimes strike his wife without incurring public disapproval, whereas the Christian Armenian husband could not.[15] In general, then, it appears that Christian wives were better off than Muslim wives. Although the social implications of this may be important, they have not been carefully investigated. Neither has there been much study of the origins of these differences.

The Muslim practice of permitting marriage between first and second cousins had both costs and benefits. The main benefit was that property could be kept within an extended family household instead of being divided and fragmented. However, psychological inbreeding through cousin marriage may be harmful, in that it may reinforce undesirable thought and behavior patterns. The Christian prohibition on such cousin marriage forced people to seek mates outside their most intimate circle, bringing "fresh blood"—and personalities—into the family.

But now it is time to rejoin the newlyweds.

4.

MARRIED LIFE AND CHILDBIRTH

A good Armenian village hars was industrious, respectful, and *hamest,* "unassuming." She was aware of the vital role of badeev and did nothing to bring gossip on herself or to cast a cloud on her family. The conditions under which she lived were somewhat harsh, perhaps, but she endured them because she believed it was necessary to win respect for herself, her husband, her family, and her household. By her unselfish devotion and hard work, she also brought badeev to her maternal family. The good fortune of her husband's family was her good fortune. Illness, tragedy, poor harvests, or individual bad judgment affected the lives of each and every person in the household. She learned to look after the best interests of the household and to look on her sisters-in-law and brothers-in-law as extensions of herself.

When the wedding festivities had come to an end and the visiting relatives had departed, the new hars began her *nor harsnutiun*—the period of being the junior wife in the gerdastan. It was a difficult time for the new bride, but it was a vital aspect of the rite of passage from girl to woman.[1] Like wedding customs, the customs of nor harsnutiun varied considerably from region to region, and certainly were much more rigidly observed in rural areas than in towns. (Indeed, some of the Detroit informants stressed that town girls simply could not adjust to the difficult life of the village bride; a village girl who married into a town family, on the other hand, could look forward to comparative ease and social freedom.) Furthermore, in the very nature of things, the extent and severity of nor harsnutiun was influenced by the personalities of the individuals within any given household.

In general, any daughter-in-law knew, upon entering a village gerdastan, that she would be expected to perform all of the usual female tasks, as well as several chores reserved for her as the woman with the least status. (Most informants, however, indicated that she did not cook; in Amasia, at least, this was a privilege reserved for the mother-in-law [Informant 46].) From her wedding day, the lower half of her face was constantly veiled—in most villages, for at least a year. Furthermore, whenever she left the house, she was completely enveloped in a sheetlike garment which revealed only her eyes. In some villages, the new wife was required always to keep her head and face not only veiled but tightly wrapped. She was not permitted to speak to anyone except the children, and even that was possible only when she was alone with them. Informant 18, from Khorsana village, and Informant 26, from Hakusdun, both described this period of silence, called *moonch*, as "the bride swallowed her tongue."[2] She could speak with her husband only when they were alone, but there were few opportunities for privacy.

Informants from different areas said that the mother-in-law usually relaxed the rule of silence when the daughter-in-law's first child was born, giving her a gift and saying, "Speak, my daughter" (Informants 1, 22, 23, 42, 46). Thereafter the young wife could answer when she was spoken to. It was entirely possible, however, that she might live in the same house with brothers- and father-in-law and never be permitted to converse with them. Even though she might not actually be forbidden to speak to the men, many village daughters-in-law felt that not speaking showed sacrifice and respect. Periods of five, ten, or even more years were not uncommon for this period of silence in the villages,[3] and in many areas the daughter-in-law continued to wear a partial veil.

A sampling of responses from the Detroit informants illustrates that the young wife's experience was conditioned more by the family into which she married than by the area in which she lived. Informant 24, from Aralez, in the Van region, indicated that the length of silence was determined by the size of the family—the greater the number, the longer the period. Her paternal uncle's wife, whose children were older than the informant, still did not speak with her brothers-in-law. Informant 43, from the town of Van itself, said that the new hars could speak only to children. However, her particular duties were simple ones: she kissed the hands of her elders and visitors who entered the house, and she poured water for those guests to wash their hands. Informant 5, from Kharzeet, on the other hand, remembered that the young wife had to wash her father-in-law's feet when he came home from the fields and prepare his bedding for the night. She kissed the hands of the priest and godfather. She also could not speak except to young children, who then carried her message to the elders. In some of the village households the wife occasionally was given a measure of freedom after the birth of her first baby, but not necessarily so. She waited until her mother-in-law released her, and she did not receive a gift at this time.

All of the informants from the Moush area who described the daughter-in-law's duties agreed that at first she could speak only to the children, but the periods mentioned ranged from one month (Informant 1, from Erzunga) to four years (Informant 3, from Karaghil). The latter informant also said that his own mother voluntarily had not spoken for seven years, out of modesty and respect for her in-laws. All also generally agreed that the junior wife had to kiss the hands of visitors and fetch the slippers and clean the shoes of her father- and mother-in-law. Informants 4 and 45 said that she had to help her father-in-law get ready for bed; Informants 4 and 17 also said that she had to wash his feet. Informant 1, however, remarked that while it was considered a matter of respect and honor to hand the towel to her mother- and father-in-law when they washed their hands, the young wife was not required to do so.

Veiling practices were more diverse. Informant 4 remembered that the new daughter-in-law's veil, which she wore until her first baby, started just below her eyes. Informant 45, on the other hand, said that at her marriage the bride wore two veils, but only one afterwards, and the one was so thin that her face was visible. She wore this veil until she had a child or until someone died in the family.

Interviews with informants from the Caesarea area are interesting because the informants themselves were so aware of the changes that were occurring in the traditional behavior. Informants 7 and 42 agreed that the young wife helped her father-in-law get ready for bed and then stood, hands folded across her breast, until dismissed. Informant 7 said that she also helped him dress in the morning. Informant 2, however, specifically said that while at one time the new daughter-in-law had been expected to help her father-in-law get ready for bed and stand at attention until she was dismissed by her mother-in-law, this was no longer true in the informant's time. Furthermore, her own mother had not spoken to her father-in-law or brother-in-law for ten years after her marriage, but Informant 2 spoke to her own mother-in-law after only six months. She also went unveiled, though she did wear a babushka over her hair.

Informants from the Kughee area confirmed that the new wife's life tended to be easier in the towns or large villages than in the rural regions. Informant 26, from the small Kughee village of Hakusdun, said that the junior daughter-in-law covered her face and could not talk to adults until her first child was two or three years old. She poured water for visitors and elders when they washed their hands, standing humbly by with her head bowed during the process. She opened the door and stood respectfully when anyone entered or left the house, and she washed the feet of the men in the family as they came in from the fields. She cleaned their shoes, mended their stockings, and helped the oldest male to get dressed. However, Informant 25, from the town of Kughee, remembered that the new wife poured water over the hands of her father- and mother-in-law as they washed, but only for a week. Her own mother had worn a veil and had not spoken to her brothers-in-law for sixteen years, but after 1908, the veil and keeping silence were no longer required. She herself spoke to everyone except her father-in-law. The informant added that when men returned to Kughee after a short stay in America, they encouraged the changing of these things, even in the villages.

On the other hand, two final examples show that the size of a settlement cannot always be an accurate guide to the strength of the traditions observed there. Informant 9, from Govdun, which was not a small village, spoke rather bitterly of the new wife's life, saying that she was relegated to a corner of the house even after sleeping with her new husband for three nights. Finally she was brought into the family grouping after she washed the feet of the patriarch and matriarch. If there were other male members in the family, she washed their feet, too. She set the table, made the bread, waited on the men's table, and then cleared away and set the table for the women. She helped her father-in-law into his night things, then stood until he dismissed her. In the morning, she was the first one up. She helped her father-in-law with his clothes and held the towel for both her mother- and father-in-law to dry themselves when they washed. Yet Informant 41, from Karakehoy, a small village, described rather liberal conditions: the new wife was unveiled in the house, though she did put on her veil when visitors came. She kissed the hands of visitors only for the first five or six days, and she was not expected to wash anyone's feet.

Once the wife had successfully completed her long period of initiation, she became a full member of the extended family, enjoying its rights and privileges. If her husband in time became the head of the household, she became the matriarch, with control over daughters-in-law, sons, and grandchildren—and if she survived her husband, she might become head of the household and be obeyed by the entire family, sons and all.[4]

Pregnancy and Childbirth

The Armenian household needed the help of many hands to support itself. Children were loved and welcomed, although by no means only for their economic contribution. Many Armenian folktales tell of the great desire for children: no matter how comfortably the characters are situated, their happiness is incomplete because they are childless. Several writers have suggested that the desire for children ultimately was associated with beliefs concerning the soul. The Armenians believed that the soul left the body at death and roamed, finding peace only as respect and prayers were offered at the grave. If a couple were childless, who would care for their graves?[5] Other scholars associate the need for children with the remnants of a family cult. The grave of the father, in particular, was held in great reverence and was certain to receive much attention; masses were said for the deceased, good works were performed in his name, and incense was burned on Saturday night on the home fire as prayers were recited. The village priest gave special blessings at the graveside at least on Merelotz, the Monday after Easter.[6] Because daughters eventually left their paternal home for their husbands' households, a man's sons bore the primary responsibility for maintaining these observances and heading the household after his death.

Pregnancy and the bearing of children—especially sons—gave the Armenian woman status as a wife and mother, reinforced her husband's manhood, and provided against her husband's eventual death. The newly married Armenian village girl thus ordinarily hoped to become pregnant as soon as possible; if she did not, she might resort to whatever the local women recommended as a cure for infertility. Informant 28, from the village of Palou in the Kharpert region, described two such remedies.[7]

> To cure a barren woman, take black sheep's wool which has never been washed and mix it with soft pig's lard. Then mix together dried cloves and *zungsefeil* [?] and add a single chick pea. Combine this with the mixture of wool and lard. Then take blue thread which has never been washed and bind it around the mixture until it forms a little egg. Next, grind *jekem* [?] and work it until it becomes gummy; spread it over the formed egg. Place this egg in the barren womb and leave it for twenty-four hours. Do this for each of seven days.
>
> After seven days, bathe the woman in hot water and place her on the ground with her face to the floor. Let the midwife stretch her back with her fingers to make it broader. When she feels that this has been accomplished, let her place the woman's feet on her own shoulders and jerk her several times so that if the pelvic girdle [uterus?] is tilted, it will fall into place where it belongs.
>
> Then grind together cloves, zungsefeil, and incense; mix them

with black tar and spread the mixture on a piece of cloth that has never been washed. Quickly pass the cloth through a fire and place it on the woman's back. Place a similar preparation above the womb.

Next let the midwife take a hen's egg and partially cook it in lukewarm water. Mix soft lard and wool of the black sheep, wrap the mixture around the egg, and place it in the woman's womb. When the egg is removed, the husband sleeps with his wife, and they should enjoy success.

Let the midwife have the woman lie with her face to the floor, and, with her fingers, manipulate the woman's skin, pushing it and moving it around until the pelvic girdle [uterus?] falls where it belongs. Then let the midwife rub the woman's back thoroughly with raki. Meanwhile, mix incense and *meadegeen* gum or black tar until they are very sticky. Place a piece of blue paper upon which many needlepoints are made in raki. Then spread the gummy mixture on the blue paper and place it on the back of the woman; let it remain there until it falls off of its own accord, taking away with it all pain.

Two or three weeks later, if the woman feels that her period is about to start, repeat this procedure.

V. H. Bdoyan reports that in some extended family households a substitute male family member might try to impregnate a barren wife, but no Detroit informant mentioned this practice.[8]

If all these measures failed, the couple might adopt a baby. According to Informant 16, from Kharpert, the adopting mother would put the baby under her dress at the neck, guide it downward, and pick it up again at the bottom of her hem—a symbolic enactment of birth that formalized the adoption. In any case, her husband—unlike a Muslim husband—could not divorce her for failure to conceive.

The strong desire for children was accompanied by equally strong fears and taboos associated with pregnancy. Most Armenians—particularly village women—believed in the existence of malevolent spirits called *al* or *alk*. Often even those individuals who insisted that they did not believe in the alk used charms to protect themselves. When a woman conceived, the family and community saw her as especially vulnerable to evil spirits and in need of special protection and sympathy. She was allowed to eat what she liked, but discouraged from drinking cold water, since, according to Informant 46, it was believed that cold water would cause her uterus to contract prematurely.

Some informants had not heard of alk, but they did mention taboos. Informant 1, from Erzunga, recited a whole list of them: a pregnant woman should not stretch to reach for something because she would entangle the umbilical cord and choke the fetus; she should not raise her arms too high or she would bear an abnormal child; she should not stand in front of a mirror because it would cause the child to move and bring possible complications; she should not stand in front of animals because the child would move in such a way that it would be abnormal.

Births normally occurred at home with the village midwife in attendance. While most Armenian women gave birth on their knees, Informants 12 and 39 said that others stooped or squatted. Sometimes the laboring woman pressed her sides as she bore down (Informant 4); others walked back and forth during labor (Informant 24). According to Informant 26, from Hakusdun, the husband felt amot and escaped from the house while his wife was giving birth, and usually all men and children were sent out of the house during this time.

When the child was born, the midwife pressed the blood in the umbilical cord toward him and stretched the freshly cut cord itself toward his face, smearing his cheeks with his own blood. The blood remained until the child's first bath, its purpose being to ensure that he would have rosy cheeks (Informants 4, 28). If the child were a boy, the family might distribute nuts and raisins to the community (Informant 5, from Kharzeet), but nothing special was done to celebrate a girl's birth. According to Informant 15, from Zeitoun, if the newborn child were defective, the midwife "didn't keep it alive." She merely told the family that the child had died at birth. This seldom happened, but the practice was socially accepted.

Immediately after the birth, the attending women either rubbed the baby with salt or bathed it in salt water. Sometimes they rubbed the whole body except the eyes, ears, mouth, and genitals, and sometimes only the joints. They left the baby in this condition for a period ranging from a few hours to three days, according to Informants 5, 15, and 26. Armenians believed that salt toughened the body, enabling the child to endure extremes of heat and cold; that it prevented colds; and that it discouraged perspiration and body odor. Informant 41, from Karakehoy, could not recall the particulars about salting the newborn, but he did remember that when someone behaved dishonorably it was said that he had not "seen salt."

The afterbirth was carefully buried, frequently under the threshold to keep it away from the pawing of animals (Informant 16). It was considered a sin to throw it away. The dried umbilical cord, on the other hand, might be disposed of in several different ways. Informant 5 remembered that it was stuck to the ceiling, but Informant 41 said that it was either thrown into the river or buried where people could not step on it. Others believed that the umbilical cord should be buried in a place associated with the family's ambition for the newborn child. Informant 28 said that if the cord were buried near a school, the child would become a scholar, if close to the marketplace, he would become a wealthy merchant. Informants 2, 16, 25, and 26 all said that if the cord were dropped quietly in the church, he would become a singer. Informant 36, from Kurdbelem, said that it was buried near the inside wall of the house, insuring that the child would be a homebody; Informant 2, from Fenesé, said that a girl's cord was buried in the pag so that she would be a homemaker, but a boy's was buried outside to insure that he would be involved in the business world.

Even after a successful pregnancy and delivery, the new mother had to face more dangers. Informant 23, from Chengiler, mentioned a metal cross placed over her bed; bread placed under her pillow; and garlic, a blue bead, or a Bible placed at her side to keep away the alk. A broom also was kept at her side because it looked like a human being and thus frightened the alk away. A written source adds that images of the Virgin and sprinkling with holy water also were considered protective.[9]

According to some informants, a new mother was not allowed to leave her home for forty days, or, according to others, for fifteen days. It was bad luck for a new mother to step over someone during the forty-day period, a fear which was probably related to a specific taboo against menstruating women stepping over children and to a general avoidance of that action. Informant 12, from Kessab, said that it was believed that stepping over a child would stunt his growth; the stepper was expected to step back to his original position in order to undo the harm.

Furthermore, the mother and newborn child were in particular danger from alk for these forty days, and it therefore was essential that she never be left alone (Informant 5, from Kharzeet, and Informant 42, from Tezeli, near Yozgat).[10] She also was not given water to drink because, as Informants 15 and 26 agreed, the evil spirit could kill the new mother by snatching her liver, dipping it in water, and eating it. One safeguard was making swishing sounds with iron instruments near the stream that supplied the household's water; if the al were in the stream, the noises would prevent it from doing any damage. Informants 16 and 26, however, said that if an al merely put its hands on the woman, she would go insane and become one of the spirit's people.

Informants 16 and 47, from Kharpert, recalled that their grandfather's grandfather once caught an al who was wearing red clothes. The ancestor stuck it with a needle and made it work for the family for many years. After that the alk did not bother them any more. Informant 26 claimed actually to have seen an al—or, rather, several of them, lined up at her window. They were small, wore clothing, but were bare-headed. They had come to take her away, just as they had formerly taken away her mother and her grandmother. But she remembered how her relatives had escaped. When she, too, called on Jesus Christ, the spirits disappeared.

The newborn himself could also be in danger from alk, who might steal him, leaving behind an ugly changeling. Whenever a baby's hair and fingernails grew very rapidly, according to Informant 28, there were grounds for suspicion that he was such a changeling. Informant 9, however, asked what a poor woman could do if this happened, and then answered her own question by saying she must keep quiet and raise the child as her own.

Informants 16 and 47 described a procedure which some villagers used to ensure the newborn's well-being, particularly if its mother had a history of stillbirths. A barber, or more frequently, the grandmother, scratched the baby's back with a razor, releasing blood. Salt or sometimes henna was then rubbed on the child's back. This blood-letting procedure often was practiced through late childhood.

Informant 28 offered the information that if two women had children at approximately the same time, neither the women nor their husbands should exchange visits for forty days. If they did, they exchanged coins. For example, if the husband of one woman visited the family of the other woman, he gave her some money and she, in turn, gave him some money. If no exchange of coins occurred, the baby of the visited couple would become ill. The only way to prevent this illness was secretly to get a wet diaper of the other child, wring out the urine, and bathe the sick baby in it.

In other cases involving infertility, multiple stillbirths, or early death, desperate mothers might resort to elaborate vows in order to protect their new children. Informant 47 personally vowed that if the child with whom she was pregnant lived, she would go to seven different houses and beg a piece of blue cloth from each of them to make it a dress. Forty days after her successful delivery, she did as she had promised, and in fact, for seven years she dressed her little boy in blue and did not cut his hair. According to her, some mothers vowed to go to seven houses and beg for silver, from which they would then have an earring made for the child's right ear. After seven years, the child would be taken to a church, where the priest would give him his first haircut. If she were wealthy enough, she had the hair weighed and made an offering of a corresponding amount of money. Informant 48, from Harseg village, also said that a woman who had had to wait for a long time before producing a healthy male child might feed him a piece of wolf liver in order to make him fearless.

As a rule, especially in the extended family, bathing the baby was the privilege of the grandmother, while the mother fetched soap, water, and towels. Carefully, the grandmother manipulated the baby's body, hoping to insure strength and regular features for her grandchild. Meanwhile, according to Informant 22, from Sepastia, she chanted:

> May you have a long neck.
> May you have black, black eyes.
> May you have a round face.
> Let there be a tiny nose.

While the child was still wet, the grandmother stretched his left leg, bringing it to the right side, and then the right leg to the left side. She treated his arms similarly, and then massaged the baby along the back of his neck, encouraging the muscles to stretch. Finally, picking him up by his feet, she held him upside-down and shook him to get rid of the water in his lungs, again singing or chanting. Informants 2, 14, 15, 24, 25, 36, and 42 all remembered the same verses:

> Shake off the water.
> May you have a long neck.
> Carry flesh—be robust.

Informant 16 substituted "may the water jump off of you" for the first line, and Informant 9 added another verse:

> May you have long arms.
> May you have a long stature.

Finally, the grandmother wrapped the baby in a towel and, together with his mother, dressed him.

Baptism

Babies were bathed daily from the day they were born until baptism, which ordinarily might occur anywhere from three to eight days (Informants 4, 16, and 36) to forty days after birth. In unusual situations—for example, if the child were a long-awaited boy— baptism might be delayed a year or more, until special conditions were met. Informant 12, from Kessab, mentioned that sometimes the mother vowed she would take the child to a certain church on a special holiday. The villagers accompanied the mother and child to the hill or the area where the church was situated. They slept and ate outdoors; in the morning, they had an open-air church ceremony, sacrificed a lamb, made *hereseh,* a special porridge of barley and lamb, and sang, danced, and celebrated before returning home.

Even in ordinary circumstances, baptism was and is a very serious rite in the Armenian family. By the end of the nineteenth century, the ceremony usually took place in church, although in medieval Armenia it was performed at home, at the toneer.[11] The new mother was seldom if ever present because she could not leave the house for forty days. Instead, the midwife, accompanied by the godfather, godmother, paternal and maternal family members, and neighbors carried the child to the church. Often this was the first time the maternal grandparents saw their grandchild. It was required that the godfather fast so that he could take communion. During the ceremony, the child was immersed in water three times.[12] At the completion of the ceremony, he was immediately confirmed by the priest, who anointed every part of his body with holy oil. The priest then blessed the clothing of the child, which traditionally was furnished by the godfather, although this custom was not rigidly observed. After the ceremony, the procession returned to the family home to celebrate. The new mother, frequently in a kneeling position, kissed the godfather's hand; only then was the child returned to her arms.[13]

In some areas, when the child was next bathed after baptism, the bath water was not discarded indiscriminately because it contained traces of *mehron,* "holy oil." Informant 25 said that it was thrown on the fuel supply to be burned eventually. Informants 16, 23, and 26 poured this water over their favorite flowers so that they would flourish. At any rate, it was necessary to discard the oil in a place where neither hand nor foot could touch it (Informants 4, 10).

The baby was kept in the house for forty days after baptism. Informant 25 said that if it were essential that he be taken out, bread was wrapped and placed with him.

Comparisons

It is difficult to compare Armenian married life with that of other peoples in eastern Europe and the Near East because very little material on the subject has been published, about either the Armenians or other peoples. Anthropologists have rarely stayed long enough in a community or mastered the language well enough to make reliable observations on intimate aspects of family life. However, on the basis of scattered materials, it is possible to find a few parallels between the customs and beliefs of the Armenians and their neighbors.

The practice of initiating a new bride in an extended family household by giving her humiliating jobs was found even after World War II among the Serbs and Turks.[14] Among these people too it was considered honorable for young brides to endure humiliation. The belief that mother and child were in danger during the first forty days after birth was widespread in eastern Europe and the Near East and, of course, had some foundation in fact, given the dangers of puerperal fever and postpartum psychosis in the mother, as well as of various infantile diseases.[15] As for the evil spirits, the Persians also believed that an *al* might kill a new mother by taking her liver and passing it through water, and so they forbade her to drink water during the forty days. They also associated the *al* with the color red. Similar beliefs were found among most of the peoples of the Caucasus. The Sumerians, Babylonians, Hebrews, and ancient Greeks believed in similar evil female beings.[16]

The Persians would also disguise a long-awaited boy as a girl, leaving his hair uncut for seven years, and then contribute the weight of the cut hair in gold to a religious institution. They too would massage an infant's nose "to make it straight."[17] The ritual of adopting a child by slipping it under the dress from neck through to the hem was practiced by the Muslim Arabs of Palestine in the 1920s.[18]

It was a widespread Near Eastern custom to rub salt, mixed either with oil or water, on a newborn baby, and to justify this action by saying it would "toughen" the child and make it "modest." This practice is mentioned in the Old Testament (Ezek. 16:4). In thirteenth-century England it was customary to rub salt on a newborn, and in the sixteenth century a priest would put salt on a child's mouth at baptism. Salt has been widely used for protection against the evil eye in Europe and the Near East in modern times. The rationale for these customs is uncertain. Perhaps, since people in the area used salt to preserve meat, they reasoned that salt would protect the flesh of the baby.[19]

5.

CHILD REARING

The successful functioning of the Armenian peasant household was dependent upon each family member's acceptance of the supremacy of the family group, respect for authority, and recognition of the necessity for hard physical labor and self-denial. Rural Armenian child-rearing practices were designed—sometimes quite consciously—to ensure that each addition to the household learned to fit in and contribute to its survival. On the negative side, one can say that because of its structure and function, the gerdastan perpetuated peasant status; it did not and could not encourage personal ambition and risk-taking. On the other hand, the shared responsibility in the extended family household made it necessary for each adult to become vitally interested in the welfare of all of the children. Ideally, at least, the gerdastan offered its members emotional, physical, and economic security in the midst of a hostile environment.

The child's initiation into the family structure and household values in a sense was symbolized by his name.[1] Unlike some groups, Armenians had no taboo against naming a child after a living person. On the contrary, they felt that such a practice increased the lifespan of the individual and, of course, perpetuated his name. Middle names were rare, and nicknames were most frequently simply shortened forms of the first name: Mariam, Maro; Sarkis, Sako; Garabed, Garo; Armenag, Armen; Arusiag, Arus. Sometimes the diminutive form of the name was used for such a long time that it stuck in adulthood: Vahan, Vanig; Mardiros, Mardig; Khatch, Khatchig.

Names were chosen to emphasize desirable personality traits or qualities: Aznive, "gracious"; Makrouhi, "woman who likes cleanliness"; Zevart, "gay"; Hamest, "modest"; Haiganoush, "sweet Armenian woman"; Isquhee, "teller of the truth"; Vartuhee, "lovely as a rose"; Garabed, "pioneer"; Hamayak, "clever"; Jirair, "strong and active man"; Hrach, "one who has fiery, bright, or clear eyes"; Kurken, "small wolf." Biblical names, or names associated with Christian holidays, saints, and martyrs were also popular: Bedros, Peter; Boghos, Paul; Mariam, Mary; Hovhannes, John; Avedis, Evangel; Kapriel, Gabriel; Mgurdich, Baptist; Nshan, Mark; Hripsime, a nun who was martyred in Armenia and for whom the most holy of shrines is named; Hampartzoum, Ascension; Harutiun, Resurrection; Mardiros, Martyr.

Some stemmed from even more ancient times: Vahagn, a god among the pre-Christian dieties; Anahit, an ancient Armenian goddess; Mihran, the sun god. One might include here names drawn from the natural world as well: Arpine, "rising sun"; Arshaloys, "daybreak"; Astghig, "small star"; Zovinar, "lightning without thunder"; Lorig, "quail"; Lucine, "moon"; Manushag, "violet"; Zepure, "pleasant breeze"; Shushan, "lily"; Tzaghig, "flower"; Aghavnee, "pigeon"; Vart, "rose"; Oski, Oskinaz, or Oskehtel, "gold"; Elmas, "pearl."

Historical references are many: Satenig, an Armenian princess; Dikran, for Tigranes, the Great King of Kings, 95–55 B.C.; Haig, founder of Haiastan (Armenia); Bakrat, a dynasty of Armenian kings of the eighth to ninth centuries A.D.; Raffi, a famous nineteenth-century writer; Parantzem, the wife of King Arshag of Armenia; Zabelle, thirteenth-century Armenian princess; Aram, father of King Ara; Ardashes, a king of Armenia in 189 B.C., who revolted against the Greeks; Ashod, an Armenian king; Dertad, the Armenian king who accepted Christianity in 301 A.D.; Hamazasp, one of the generals of Vartan; Antranig (for a firstborn), General Antranig; Garo, Armen Garo; Soseh, Antranig's wife; Vartan, defender of the Armenian Christian nation against Zoroastrian warriors.

Some names designated geographical landmarks: Araxee, Arax River; Massis, a folk reference to Ararat; Dikranouhee, Dikranagert, the capital city of Tigranes, the great king of Armenia; Ara, for the hero Ara Keghetzig, in whose name the plains of Ararat are named; Ani, the ancient Armenian capital city. A few names were concerned with social position. Since Muslims held all the important places, it is not surprising that some Turkish first names appear, such as Sultan, Khatoon ("lady"), and Aga Bob; native Armenian ones were Takouhee ("queen"); Arshag, for a king of Armenia; Azad ("free" man); Diran ("one who rules").

In later life, of course, informal naming practices might result in the attachment of a descriptive epithet. Some epithets merely acknowledged the trade or profession of the individual: *ketchejee* Vartan ("feltmaker" Vartan); *marangose* Arsen ("carpenter" Arsen); *tertzag* Aram ("tailor" Aram); *djagharchban* Krikor ("miller" Krikor); *hamamjee* Levon ("bath attendant" Levon); *pasdurmajee* Kapriel ("dried beef curer" Kapriel); *chobanots* Hrant ("shepherd" Hrant); *fooroonjee* Gaspar ("baker" [tender of ovens] Gaspar). Other nicknames, such as *topal* ("lame") Levon; *mazod* ("hairy") Mariam; *sheel* ("cross-eyed") Garo; *guduh bagas* ("lacking seeds or sense") Mardig; and khool ("deaf") Armen, indicated undesirable qualities.

A masculine name was feminized by adding a suffix: -*ouhee* changes Azad to Azadouhee; Dikran to Dikranouhee; Armen to Armenouhee; Berj to Berjouhee; Diran to Dirouhee; -*anoush* changes Haig to Haiganoush.

Infant Care

Armenian infants were swaddled—a process called *khndaght*—with their legs held together to encourage straight limbs. Informant 14, from Gavra village, Sepastia region, talked about two wraps: *tevlot,* used for the arms and above the waist, and *kovlot,* used for the legs and areas below the waist. Informant 15, from Zeitoun, mentioned a third cloth known as the *khumash* or *ver-akash,* which could be adjusted and was wrapped around the child's middle, keeping him securely in place and permitting no movements of fingers and toes. Informant 16, from Kharpert, also said that the navel was tightly bound to prevent a protruding stomach. The swaddling was most rigorous when the child was put to sleep; his limbs were not so tightly bound during the day (Informants 11, 25).

The swaddled child was placed in a wooden cradle with some provision for disposing of urine and feces. Informant 15 described placing a light cane tube to carry the urine through a hole in the cradle into a container below; Informant 36, from Kurdbelem, Gayve district, knew of cradles with holes placed beneath the lower part of the baby's body. Wastes ran into a cup beneath the hole. Most households, however, simply lined the cradle with fine absorbent sand, which might then be covered with a cloth (Informant 17, from Kharadigin, near Erzunga). Wet sand was easily scooped out for disposal. (According to Informant 26, from Hakusdun, a piece of cotton was dipped in paraffin and placed over the penis of a boy or under the buttocks of a girl to keep the diaper dry.) Informant 12, from Kessab, spoke of fetching sand from the mountains, but Informant 4 said that most households simply bought large quantities every fall and stored it in petakner in the maran along with winter food supplies. The sand was then warmed and spread in the cradle as it was needed. The baby was kept on this warm sand until he was completely toilet-trained, even if it took two years. As he got older, however, he was put on the sand at night, but not so much during the day. Some Armenians believed the sand not only saved labor but that its strength and power were transmitted to the child. However, just before the World War I massacre, according to Informant 1, the use of sand was slowly disappearing.

Armenians toilet-trained their children as early as possible, since living conditions were crowded and laundering was difficult, especially during the long winter. Although Informant 4 indicated that the grandmother took charge of toilet-training, no one else agreed, and indeed, this training seems specifically to have been the mother's responsibility. Usually the mother would encourage the infant to urinate near her feet when it was only a few months old. She sat on the ground, the soles of her feet together and knees slightly flexed. Then she either held it in a sitting position, supporting its buttocks, or in an upright position, spreading its legs apart (Informant 48). Other informants described variations of this method. Informant 17 said that mothers started toilet-training early by holding the baby over a pan, and several others indicated that the baby was held, his back to his mother, perhaps with his legs held apart, over a container on the ground and kept there until he performed. Informant 48 said that an older child who refused to cooperate in toilet-training might be swatted on the buttocks with a straw broom, but no other informant confirmed that there was any punishment. Rather, Armenians believed that a child who had difficulty in controlling his urine suffered from a weak back.

The baby's cradle was anchored to two strong, floor-to-roof house posts situated close together, thus forming a pocket. Cushions were placed at the bottom of the pocket, and the high sides served to hold the child inside. A long tie or rope was attached; by pulling gently on it, one could rock the cradle. Several informants remembered that wooden cradles were always swinging in their households, anchored to the sturdy pillars. When the child no longer wet himself or when he was about two years old, he was removed from the cradle and slept either with an older sibling or in a bed roll by himself.

Young children rocked the cradle while the mother was out in the fields, although Informants 14, from Gavra, 40, from Tortan village, near Kemakh, and 48, from Harseg village, near Kharpert, said that sometimes a cradle post with three sticks was made and the child placed in it under a shady tree until it needed to be nursed. Sometimes hassocks were set up in the fields where the mother was working. Informant 17 mentioned an arrangement whereby the baby could rock himself while everyone worked. Other children also might carry the baby piggyback to the fields to be nursed if necessary (Informants 17, 40). (Mothers normally carried their babies in their arms, not on their backs.) In some village households, the mother nursed the baby and then went to the fields. If she were not too busy, she returned and nursed again at midday. Otherwise, the older children brought the baby to her.

Most Armenian babies were nursed for at least two years, and a four-year period was not uncommon if the mother did not become pregnant again. One or more procedures might be followed to ensure that the new mother had an adequate supply of milk. In all cases, the new mother's breasts were emptied before the child was first put to them. Gentle massage of the breasts was also recommended. Informant 14 recalled that she was also told to keep her shoulders warmly covered in order to stimulate her flow of milk, and she added that a mixture of honey and lukewarm water was placed on her baby's tongue two or three times in order to teach him to swallow before he began to nurse.

Foods such as soups, meats, and sweets were considered helpful in producing milk. Although most of the Detroit informants indicated that spicy, sour, bitter, and peppery foods should be avoided because these would cause distress to the baby, Informant 48 felt that eating any and all foods from the very start would accustom the baby to unusual tastes and would prevent feeding problems later on. Mothers with insufficient milk to satisfy their babies could resort to homemade baby foods, such as cooked and crushed raisins (Informant 44). All informants on this issue agreed that in hot weather the breasts should be washed with cool water before nursing, in order to make the milk more digestible.

It was not unusual for a sister-in-law to nurse the baby if the mother were out of the house and the baby cried, but if the mother or household women could not, a wet nurse who had sufficient supply undertook the job. Such a woman was never paid in money, but in exchanges of food or services. Informant 1, from Erzunga, said, however, that if the wet nurse had a girl and the family had a boy, the children could not grow up and marry each other because they had drunk the same milk. Informant 44, from Kughee, added that villagers used the tiny horns of a calf as a milk bottle to feed the occasional child who had neither mother's milk nor a wet nurse. Informant 44 also reported that in her native area, if the evil eye had caused a mother's milk to dry up, she was encouraged to make a pilgrimage to a holy fountain called *Gahtnaghpeur* ("the Milk Fountain"). Together with the firstborn daughter of another woman, the milkless mother walked to Gahtnaghpeur, remembering never to look behind her. When she reached the fountain, she dipped a piece of bread into the water and ate it. Then she washed her breasts with the water. Immediately they would swell with milk, and she would happily return home to her baby.

If, on the other hand, a mother's milk were very abundant and her child a poor nurser, particularly in the early days when his sucking instinct was not well developed, every attempt was made to share the milk supply with another child in the community. According to Informant 44, if this expedient proved to be impossible, a newborn puppy was put to the mother's breasts to empty them and keep her lactating for the day when the baby would nurse strongly. Informant 4, from Vardo-Gundemir, said that another remedy was to run a comb over the full breasts to break up the milk glands, giving the mother some comfort when the child did not nurse well.

Generally a mother tried to nurse the baby whenever it was hungry, but the Detroit informants repeatedly said that it was not desirable to pick the child up as soon as it began to cry. Some crying "opened and stretched" the child's lungs—though the informants did admit that children were nursed more quickly at night because their crying would disturb the entire household. Apparently all mothers avoided taking a child into their own beds for nursing. Because the mother was so often exhausted and the baby so tightly swaddled, there was a real danger that she might roll over and suffocate the child. During the day the baby was picked up to nurse; at night the mother, having no chair to sit on, would kneel beside the cradle, tip it toward her, bend over, and offer her breast (Informants 14, 23, 25, 35).[2]

Apparently nursing was done in private whenever possible. Informants 9 and 12 said that nursing in front of others was not shameful, but Informants 26 and 40 disagreed, remarking that open breast-feeding was unusual and women avoided it when they could. In fact, Informants 1 and 2 said that a mother did not even sing to her baby while nursing, but only when he was ready to sleep, and Informants 4 and 26 remarked that even then it was amot for elders to hear the lullaby.

When the mother became pregnant with her next child, she stopped nursing, believing that continuing would harm the fetus

(Informants 44, 48). Most mothers weaned their children simply by systematically reducing the number of breast-feedings; sometimes the sister-in-law completely took over caring for the child during this period "so that he would not smell his mother's milk." Meanwhile, the mother reduced her milk supply by cutting down on liquids, binding her breasts, and perhaps placing cold compresses on them (Informants 4, 40). According to Informant 44 from Kughee, in several areas a woman would wrap pickled cabbage leaves in a towel and place it on her breast; Informant 17, from Kharadigin, said soap was used instead of cabbage leaves.

If a child were difficult to wean, his mother might spread red pepper (Informants 44, 48) or ink (Informant 44) on her breasts, meanwhile telling the child that it was *kukh,* "unpleasant." Placing "bad-tasting stuff or black wooly stuff" on the nipple was mentioned by Informants 1, 25 and 34; Informant 9 said that sometimes a woman put a bar of soap in her armpit. According to Informant 48, however, the one foolproof method of weaning was for the mother to wear a small bag of dried mint around her neck, but this was seldom resorted to because it was said that the woman would never be able to nurse again. Finally, many informants mentioned the use of pacifiers made out of gauze wrapped around dried mulberries, ground raisins, madzoon and honey, or prepared sweets.

As the infant grew, his mother prepared him to accept solid food by chewing her own food to soften it and then placing it in the child's mouth with her own spoon, but the age at which he was expected to feed himself varied considerably. Informant 40 placed this independence as early as one year, but at the other extreme, Informant 14 said that a child should be between two and three years old. One informant did remark that a child could be so *jarbeeg,* "clever," that he could "fill his stomach" at one year; Informants 22 and 25 agreed that eighteen months was the ideal age.

Almost everywhere in Armenia, when the child cut his first tooth, hadig was prepared and family friends were invited to share in the festivities. In some areas, this was the only celebration of the infancy period.[3] The household women boiled kernels of whole wheat and then added raisins, almonds, dried and salted chick peas, and candies. It was hoped that just as the grain multiplied in cooking, so would the child's teeth. (This kind of dish, called *kolliva* in Greek, *frumenty* in English, and *kutia* in Russian, symbolized regeneration and had many ritual uses in eastern Europe and the Near East.)[4] Guests sometimes brought gifts to the child, but almost always took home some hadig (Informant 16, from Kharpert). Sometimes, instead of inviting guests to the house, the family sent hadig to the neighbors (Informants 2, 14, 15).

The child was placed on a sheet together with various items: a gun, a book, a pair of scissors, a comb, and so on. Hadig was sprinkled over the child's head while everyone waited to see what he would reach for first. The item chosen foretold the baby's future vocation (Informants 8, 39, 46). Informants 25 and 45 described a similar event, except that hadig containing raisins, nuts, and money was placed on a small screen, which was then placed on the child's head. With the movement of his head, the screen soon fell, spilling its contents. If the child reached first for the money, it was believed that he would be rich.

Hadig also was used to quicken the teething process. If the child were a boy, it was strung on a thread and sewn on his cap. If the child were a girl, she wore a string of hadig as a necklace. In both instances, the baby was bathed frequently so that his teeth would issue forth just as quickly as the running water splashed (Informant 40). Informant 36 said that the hadig celebration did not occur in her native village of Kurdbelem, but she had heard that whoever saw the first tooth must buy new clothes for the baby. She also indicated that whoever saw the child's first tooth must rip apart the child's shirt in order to encourage his teeth to come just as quickly as the shirt was torn. Later, when the baby teeth were changing to permanent teeth, parents encouraged the child to throw an old tooth over his shoulder and, without looking back, say, "Go away donkey's teeth, come lamb's teeth." This custom was carried to Detroit and continued to be observed there.

Parents were not anxious for their children to walk, and usually did not hurry them to do so. However, Informant 6, from Urantz, Rushtunian district, Informant 9, from Govdun, near Sepastia, and

Informant 16, from Kharpert, said that in their villages families marked the occasion when a child first crawled or walked by offering him a variety of objects to reach for, as in the first-tooth celebration. Most other informants either recalled no special observance at that time or described a different one. In Kughee, for example, the *shekerleek* ceremony was observed with the baby's first steps. A cakelike confection with a hole in the center and red thread tied at two sides was placed around the baby's foot. The group waited to see what direction the baby would take. If he moved toward the outdoors, it was said that he would be an outsider (leave the community when he was grown). If he moved toward the inside of the house itself, they believed he would be a homebody. In another shekerleek custom reported by Informant 44, the young children of the household encircled the baby and yanked at the katah on his leg, breaking it to pieces, which they snatched and ran away with to the mountains. The women hoped that as the child matured he, too, would run exactly as fast. Informant 23, from Chengiler, near Bursa, said that when the baby walked for the first time, whomever he walked to was expected to give him a gift. Informant 48, from Harseg village, added the information that if a child were late in walking, the women tied bread around his leg and encouraged him to take a few steps. After he had done so, they untied the bread and the child would run along.

Instilling Cultural Values

On account of the lack of physical privacy in the gerdastan, the adults addressed each other rather formally, thus maintaining a certain psychological distance from each other. Family members restrained themselves not only in showing hostility, but also in expressing affection. In most parts of Armenia young parents in a gerdastan would feel constrained both from reprimanding their children and from hugging and kissing them in the presence of their elders. Fifteen of the Detroit informants clearly specified that the elders (grandparents, great-uncles, and great-aunts) were responsible for both discipline and public displays of affection to all children in the household, and only Informant 21, a man from Meghoozeek, near Erzunga, and Informant 25, a woman from Kughee, expressly denied that demonstrating parental love was amot.[5] Informant 37, a woman from Akhalkalakh, in Georgia, did remark that in her area leaving discipline to other family members was considered an old-fashioned custom.

Other informants said that while the mother could not show her love openly, the father could do so before his own mother, but not before his father and uncles (Informants 22, 39); one said that the father did not express his love for his child until it crawled (Informant 41). Informant 39 added that sometimes grandparents would say to the father, when they saw that his child needed correction, "Dghaheed khosk hasgutzoor; dghaheed mart sheeneh" ("Make your son understand reason; make your son a man"), but generally the father seems not to have been involved in discipline. One particularly touching story, however, suggests that the parents did not always restrain themselves willingly. According to Informant 45, her own father, out of respect for custom, had not expressed much affection for his children. But when his young son died, he wept, hugged the body, and cried out, "I couldn't love you when you were alive. Let me love you now." This kind of situation did not exist, of course, if the grandfather died and the household split into nuclear families.

Whether or not Armenian elders openly expressed their love for the children in their household, their educational and disciplinary practices must have fostered emotional security by combining close supervision with tolerance for children's limited capacities. A survey of the informants' responses indicates that, generally speaking, children of both sexes under the age of six were treated in much the same way, sharing responsibility for such simple tasks as pulling weeds or even, according to Informant 24, from Aralez, near Van, weaving rugs. At about seven, however, male and female duties (and privileges) became increasingly differentiated.

Girls began such jobs as sweeping the house and akhor each day, bringing water from the spring, helping to make bread and tahn, and folding and putting away the bedding in the morning. Although one woman indicated that five- and six-year-old children were responsible for the care of their younger siblings, this task generally was assigned to girls about ten years old. Not only did these older girls care for and amuse the younger ones, even carrying the tiny infants to their mothers in the fields for nursing, but the eldest child was punished if any of her charges hurt themselves (Informants 1, 2, 46). At this time too, girls learned to knit stockings and started accumulating the many pairs they would need for their trousseaus. By as early as twelve, but more commonly by fifteen, the young girl had developed real skill at the spinning wheel and the loom (Informant 14). Together with her mother and her sisters-in-law, she made, cut, and sewed textiles of various types.

Among the tasks assigned to a boy were bringing water, cutting wood, carrying wood upstairs, or (though usually only in the towns) going to the store for something which his mother needed. Girls were sometimes sent to the store when they were very young, but, like schooling away from the home village (see chap. 3, p. 71), this stopped once they reached their sixth or seventh birthdays. By the age of twelve, most Armenian village boys were skilled in harvesting and threshing; in silk-producing areas, they had also learned to grow silkworms (Informant 23, from Chengiler, near Bursa). This informant added that at about ten, girls went to the local silk factories to learn how things were done, and at twelve or thirteen, they started working there. According to Informant 44, from Kughee, in some households boys ate with the women and other young children until they were at least seven, at which time they joined the men's table. Informant 48, from Harseg village, near Kharpert, said that the ages varied from seven years old to twelve.

Throughout the many household and field tasks which these children and young people performed, they were impressed with the certainty that only by actually doing a thing would they learn how. Expressions such as "do and learn," "do it for me; learn it for yourself," "do it for me, but take it with you," and "good or bad, do it and you will perfect it" express this philosophy of acquiring skill through practice. When youngsters undertook difficult or heavy jobs, adults were there to teach, guide, and physically help. Rarely was the child expected to shoulder a responsibility beyond his capacity.

The sex role division at, roughly, age seven corresponds, again roughly, to the age at which a child of either sex was liable to being held responsible for the consequences of his own behavior. The Detroit informants, asked to respond to a question about this issue, replied with answers ranging from six years old (Informants 4, 25, for example) to as old as seventeen (Informant 10) and twenty (Informants 31, 32). Informant 15 quoted her mother as having said, "Until you are seven, your behavior is my fault; when you are seven, you are responsible for yourself." In these terms, girls matured earlier than boys. Because girls married younger, Informant 2, from Fenesé, near Caesarea, said that a girl was considered an adult by twelve; indeed, if she were not married by fifteen, she was labeled an old maid.

Between infancy and this early adulthood, however, Armenian children were thoroughly trained in acceptable codes of behavior and developed a strong awareness of the social consequences of violating them. Any adult member of a household, at any time, had the right and the responsibility of reprimanding as well as directing a younger member. Moreover, responsibility for young children was not limited to members of the immediate family. When an Armenian spoke of "our Aram" or "our Miriam," he could have been referring to a person in his village, not necessarily to one of his family, and his disciplining of the child was as welcome as discipline by a close relative. The youngster who had been taught from his earliest days to respect his elders did not resent such guidance; in any case, that he had done wrong often was communicated to his parents rather than to him, according to the notion that his parents ought to know in order to punish him appropriately.

A more positive aspect of communal supervision was that children also were taught to become aware of the needs of others and to develop compassion for the unfortunate. The duty to help others was strongest within the family, extending outward to kin, friends, and neighbors—although, according to Informant 15, Turks were outside the outermost circle of concern. The family did not teach youngsters to keep whatever they had for themselves because they had so little; instead, even the struggling family often sent bread, madzoon, or soup to even poorer families, with the children serving as messengers (Informant 15). The child not only listened to his parents but watched family members interact; he witnessed their kindness to the less fortunate and the friendships between neighbors.

Those who were stingy were called *cheengeneh* ("gypsy"), according to Informant 23, but Informant 17 pointed out that they also were not encouraged to be "open-handed" and let money seep through their fingers. Compassion was a two-edged sword. Several informants said that children were taught to help those who needed help, especially the aged, but they were also taught not to pity the handicapped, because they might bring the same affliction on themselves if they did. Pregnant women were particularly sensitive to this taboo; Informants 16 and 37 mentioned that the saying "I took pity and it came to wrap itself around my neck" was a common explanation for disasters of birth or daily living.

While all Armenian children thus were inculcated with certain broad cultural values, the village community held up different models for the "good boy" and "good girl." Informants 4, 10, 31, 32, and 46 described the ideal Armenian boy as being humble, obedient, loyal, honest, and respectful (having *harkank*); Informants 14 and 22 added that he was also expected to possess a certain degree of stubbornness (*ehnadutiun*) that would keep him from being too accepting or compliant. Other qualities particularly admired in males were those of being *achkapatz* ("wide awake" or "alert") and jarbeeg (roughly, "having the ability to profit from any given situation at any time"). "Jarbeeg" is an adjective frequently heard in Armenian speech, but it is difficult to translate. It denotes a combination of cleverness, shrewdness, intelligence, and luck. Armenians needed to be jarbeeg to stay alive in Turkey.[6] Several informants wanted their sons to be brave and willing to seek revenge; all parents wanted them to be *askasehr*, "patriotic," but they were cautious about where and when the children should express these feelings.

Education and skill at trades or business were very important for town-bred boys, but village families were more likely to value plain common sense and hard work. Informants 17, 24, and 26, for example, stressed that they wanted their sons to be good farmers, skilled at sowing, reaping, and caring for animals; Informants 17 and 24 added that high ability in school did not amount to much, but unusual performance in the fields brought a boy great esteem. What these individuals were really saying was that in the circumstances in which the Armenian people lived, even a very bright boy could go beyond the elementary grades only rarely. What did count was a few more measures of bulghur for feeding the large family in the winter ahead.

A good Armenian girl was described as being respectful, obedient, modest, chaste, and a hard worker. While a pretty face and figure were desirable, they were not essential; the girl, however, must be clean and neat. Literacy seldom enhanced her reputation, although common sense was highly valued. Indeed, some villagers considered literacy a liability in a girl because she would be able to communicate with her husband when he was away from home, and he should learn only what his parents intended for him to know. In this context, Informant 17 repeated a popular saying, "A woman who is literate will destroy the house."

An Armenian girl learned to become a dahn degeen, a "lady of the house," at her mother's side, observing and practicing the various handicrafts and household routines. At the same time, she imbibed daily lessons in modesty and ladylike behavior. She was made aware of her skirt length and of how she sat and moved; she was discouraged from spreading her legs or exercising vigorously because she might damage her hymen. "Amot eh"—"It is shameful"—was an expression she learned early, and having once been told that something was amot, she was expected never to do it again. If she failed to learn her lesson, it might be said of her, "Yerehsuh bahdratz eh" ("The veil over her face is ripped"; that is, she disregards the conventional moral code). Informant 39 said approvingly that a girl's greatest ambition was to be so good that a reputable family would select her for their bride.

Children of either sex were not supposed to know about pregnancy and birth. Informant 23 remembered that when a boy was born into the gerdastan, the adults said to her, "We found a baby brother under the grape vines." When a girl was born, they said, "We found a baby sister under the fig tree." Informants 31 and 32 said that mothers simply never explained anything about sex because it was amot, and in Informant 15's household, children were punished if they showed any curiosity about it. According to Informant 48, young girls were permitted to sit among the women and do simple tasks for them while they talked and worked, but older girls were sent away for fear they might overhear something indecent for their ears.

There was no celebration or ritual observance of any kind at menarche. Instruction about menstruation might be given by an older female relative, but only rarely by the girl's mother (Informant 1); sometimes a neighbor girl shared her knowledge. Naturally it was not uncommon for a pubescent girl, ignorant of the biological facts, to be concerned and frightened when her periods began. Informant 1 remembered crying until her sister-in-law reassured her and helped her prepare a napkin from soft cloth. This informant never spoke to her mother about the event, but she knew that her sister-in-law had done so.

The Armenian rural community commonly used more rewards than punishments in child rearing. In any case, serious disciplinary action was seldom necessary. When pressed, several informants mentioned disobedience, disrespectfulness, and dishonesty as examples of behavior requiring punishment; Informant 12 also specified avoiding work and using bad language, while Informant 17 went so far as to include punishment for a child who got himself dirty—if he were old enough to know better. The informants' responses were fairly consistent about the necessity for immediate punishment by whichever adult happened to observe the offense, but they also agreed that once the punishment had been administered, the episode was forgotten. When Informant 48 was asked if a mother ever put off disciplining a child until she thought of a meaningful punishment, the informant replied, "At the very time the child does wrong is when he should be punished. After all, who can bring her hand to strike a child once her anger is past?" In truth, Armenian adults seldom resorted to slaps or spankings, and there was general agreement that children were never spanked after the age of ten or twelve. Threats were not uncommon— Informant 39 mentioned "Abdagh muh dahm, yerehssuhd meoys goghmuh yertah" ("I'll give you such a slap that your face will go to the other side")—but no one followed through.[7]

The preferred mode of correction was to exert psychological pressures of various kinds. Some of these pressures might be called positive rather than negative. For example, physical isolation was not practiced. Where was there in the crowded household to put the child? Nor was the child simply ignored as a punishment, as is done in some American households. Rather, a child's behavior was often discussed in the family circle, with any number of individuals present at the hearing. This technique was carried to Detroit by the immigrants, who commonly discussed their American-born children with relatives, neighbors, and visitors, much to the discomfort of the children and any visiting non-Armenian friends. Moreover, instead of punishment, the mother (in a nuclear family) or grandmother (in the village gerdastan) was likely to *hamozel* ("to persuade with advice or to sweet talk"; mentioned by Informants 5, 25, 26, 34, 43) or *khuradel* ("to give a moral lesson"; mentioned by Informants 5, 7, 25, 26, 34, 36) the child. By talking to him quietly, she tried to get him to understand that his behavior brought amot upon himself and all members of his family. Favorite sayings were "Others will think less of you," "Be a good boy so that others won't talk about you; it is amot for you and amot for your family," or "Be a good boy and a hard worker so that others will see how good you are, and what an industrious and fine family you come from." In what one must suppose were particularly serious circumstances, the power of religion was available to the desperate parents. Informant 14, from Gavra village, Sepastia region, reported the following possibilities:

> If a child was frequently badly behaved, he was encouraged to go to a particular holy shrine, light a candle, and ask God to help him improve his behavior.

Another holy shrine, placed in a large field near a monastery, was noted for its power to correct bad children. The mother took her child with her to the shrine, lit a candle, and both of them prayed. Then the child turned a somersault and his bad behavior was left behind.

Most of the Detroit informants said that Armenian mothers and grandmothers often used role models as a motivation for good behavior. The moralistic stories, of course, emphasized desirable behavior through the characters,[8] but adults often also held up other family members or acquaintances for imitation. They hoped to develop *paree nakhantz* ("good jealousy"; competition) in order to stir a child to greater achievement or better behavior. The mother might say, "So-and-so is a hard worker. She wove this much cloth. Everyone says what a hard worker she is. Why don't you try to be like her?"

Perhaps surprisingly, however, very little jealousy was apparent among children within a household. Informants admitted that there was some resentment, some quarreling, and some actual fighting, but they agreed that it was uncommon. Informants 4, 5, and 7 seemed to express the consensus when they pointed out that children did not expect equality among themselves any more than they expected equality within the extended family structure.

Other Armenian child-training techniques were perhaps more psychologically damaging, at least potentially. In addition to threatening physical punishment, adults played on childish fears in order to enforce desirable behavior. Many informants remembered hearing "God will punish you if you do that," or "Be a good boy or the Kurd will get you," or "Don't go near such-and-such a place or the bear will grab you." Children commonly were taught to fear thunderstorms, Turks, the devil, wolves, and corpses.

Some households used a training technique called *zooroutznel,* which means "to make clever," but could also be translated as "teasing." Adults led the child on and then laughed at his discomfort, intending to teach him that people were not always to be trusted and that one must be wary in this world. Indeed, one must be careful not to be duped and thus become a laughingstock. Informants 2, 7, 8, 11, 15, 36, and 45 denied ever having heard of zooroutznel, but there is no doubt that the technique existed and was carried to America by at least some immigrant families. Several first-generation Armenian Americans suffered from it while growing up.

Comparisons

Ernestine Friedl found among the Greeks the practice of teasing a child so that it would not take the words and actions of others at face value. This is interesting because the Greeks, like the Armenians, took pride in their cleverness. The Persians, settled Arabs, and Sicilians also taught children to be mistrustful and clever.[9]

Throughout the Mediterranean basin families struggled to maintain their honor within the community. An important aspect of family honor was that daughters remain virgin until marriage and faithful thereafter. This has been a focus of attention for many anthropologists. According to one theory, concern about honor was strong where government was weak, and each household and clan was forced to attend to its own defense. Honor served to keep male kinsmen united, delaying the segmentation of households and clans that otherwise would have split over economic issues.[10] In any case, as long as there were few opportunities in commerce and industry, children usually had to submit to the will of family and local community. For the family and neighbors were all they had to protect them in a world full of danger. However, the Armenian had to pay for family and community support by suppressing many of his strong emotions.

There were both psychological benefits and costs in being Armenian. The benefits came from having a supportive family and friends. There was much hard work, but also there were times of joy, such as weddings. The "good" Armenian boy tended to achieve and eventually became the respected head of a large household. The "good" Armenian girl, after a difficult period as a newlywed, could look forward to being a matriarch. The cost of being Armenian was the strain of maintaining extraordinary self-control. It was necessary to be on guard against deception; to be "duped" was shameful. It was necessary to hide anger, envy, and pride. To reveal sexual desires was shameful except during a brief courtship period. Christian teachings, of course, reinforced many of the demands that Armenian elders made on their offspring. Overall, these teachings urged children to restrain proud, aggressive, envious, or lustful impulses. The Christian faith also brought consolation to those who repented having such impulses.

6.

RITUALS, BELIEFS, AND OMENS

Attitudes toward Nature

The way the Armenians thought about nature probably originated in pre-Christian times. Like many other peasants in Europe and the Near East, Armenian villagers were able to retain ancient beliefs and practices in spite of the disapproval of their church leaders. Their practices were pagan in the etymological sense: the English word "pagan" comes from Latin *paganus*, "villager." Christianity had its earliest and strongest hold in urban areas of Europe and the Near East; it was slow to root itself in the countryside. In England, for instance, there were strong rural pre-Christian survivals in the countryside as late as the seventeenth century; in the nineteenth century there were still widespread survivals of pre-Christian religion throughout the rural areas of Europe.[1] Similarly, turn-of-the-century rural Armenian customs retain traces of ancient pagan beliefs and practices, although Armenia became Christian in 301—the first national group officially to adopt the new religion. It certainly would not be correct to say that they worshiped nature or were in any sense consciously polytheistic, worshiping a plurality of deities associated with nature. Rather, many of their seasonal rituals, as well as beliefs associated with particular objects or places, are recognizably colored by survivals from the pre-Christian past, but these survivals were almost always set in a Christian context.

For example, there is no evidence that turn-of-the-century Armenians worshiped the sun, moon, or stars, although it is worth noting that remnants of ancient attitudes toward the sun may survive, even in modern America, in the characteristic Armenian expressions "areveed mehrneem" ("may I die for your sun"), "arevehd shadnah" ("may your sun [life] increase"), "achkee looysee" ("light unto your eyes"). Armenian villagers might time their activities by the motions of celestial bodies, or use images of them in amulets, but that was all.[2] What the Armenians revered most in nature were three elements: earth, water, and fire. In particular, they valued fertile soil, pure spring water, and their own hearth fire. Earth, water, and fire were essential for survival. To a lesser extent, the Armenians revered certain mountains, trees, animals, and birds, because they had qualities lacking in human beings.

Because Armenians believed that Mother Earth, the source of all good things for humans and animals, was alive and had magic power, they made divinations by it. They also had a large store of rituals to ensure the fertility of the soil—which is certainly to be expected in a country in which great masses of rocky mountain surround small patches of arable alluvium. The Armenians, however, did not regard stone as alien: it was a condensation of Mother Earth. When they removed stones from a field they stacked them alongside it, believing that to remove the stone entirely would weaken the earth. Informant 13, from Akor village, Kharpert province, said that a barren tree could be made fruitful if one placed a stone in the fork of it. Armenians also believed that certain special stones had the power to make barren women fertile and dry women give milk, heal illness, and bring rain.[3] They similarly revered mountain peaks. In the summer, while tending their flocks in the high pastures, they climbed them and offered sacrifices. For worship they might use holy caves that they found at or near the summits. Of all these peaks, snow-topped Mount Ararat was supreme, the symbol of Armenia itself, of hope and aspiration.

Armenian reverence for water, especially pure spring water, was very marked. They made artistic stone shelters and pavements around the many springs found outside their villages, and they believed that if they made a sacrifice and lit a candle at a holy spring, the water of that spring could heal eye diseases, shingles, rashes, muteness, deafness, and depressions. Like special stones, it could make barren women fertile and cause milk to flow in dry breasts. If sprinkled on gardens and fields, it could stimulate fertility and bring rain.[4]

Sometimes the Armenians personified the magic power of spring water either as a nymph or as the goddess Anahit. Anahit was a pagan deity, many vestiges of whose worship survived in Armenia in the late nineteenth century. In the Dersim area, at the confluence of the Euphrates and Aradzani rivers, the Armenians believed that a beautiful maiden, with bare breasts and the body of a fish below the waist, sat on a rock braiding her hair. They called her "our Mother Anahit." In Akor village, near the Kharpert area, there was a "healing" spring the Armenians called "Anahit's Spring." Anahit was also the patroness of childbirth. In reverence for her agents, Armenian women refrained from working on the eve of Sunday, Wednesday, or Friday. If her baby became ill, at daybreak on a Friday a woman went to collect water from all wells and fountains of the village to bathe it.[5] Manuk Abeghian confirms that Armenians, who even today believe that flowing water is holy and should not be defiled, regarded certain wells as Christian holy places, where people sacrificed hens, burned incense, and said special prayers.[6]

Since they lived in a region subject to droughts, the villagers might use magic in order to bring rain. One device was to sprinkle water from holy springs onto the fields; another was to yoke women to a plow and dig a furrow in the dry earth. Still another was to parade a female dummy called "Nuri" about the village.[7] Informant 16, from Kharpert, described what appears to be a Christianized version of this ritual. The village children made a wooden cross and dressed it in clothes and a colorful cap. Then they marched with it through the streets, singing, "From the lamp, you give us light; from the bread box, you give us bread; from the granary, you give us grain; dear God, from above, give us rain." The adults then gave the children grain and bread in the hope that God would in turn provide rain. The husband of the same informant added that another reliable method of bringing rain was to cut the head off of a Turkish corpse and throw it into a river. Bdoyan's studies confirm a variation of this gruesome practice, in which the villagers exhumed a corpse, cut off the skull, and sprinkled water on it.[8] This custom may have been inspired by the widespread ancient belief that the newly dead were thirsty. If the living satisfied the dead, perhaps God would satisfy the living.

The hearth fire, like earth and water, was linked with the female principle in Armenian thinking. Women were responsible for lighting and maintaining the fire, and, as explained in chapter 1, the hearth fire also symbolized the family and clan and was the focus of family worship. Before leaving a household, Armenians squatted before the hearth and kissed it. When a household divided, fire from the original hearth was used to light the new one.[9] Informant 2 told a story that vividly recalls the symbolic importance of the fire. During the deportation of the Western Armenians in 1915, her uncle placed her in Aleppo with some Europeans. "I am going to leave you here," he said. "If we die, there will at least be someone from our hearth who will light a fire." Certain everyday Armenian expressions also underscore this attitude: "mukhus maretzav" ("my smoke went out" [expressing exhaustion]); "seerdus guh varee" ("my heart burns" [expressing great pity or yearning for someone or something]).

Certain trees also were holy or magical in Armenian belief. Any large tree was a rarity in their deforested land, and thus likely to be associated with extraordinary or supernatural happenings. Sometimes such a tree was located just outside the village, but Informants 15, 22, and 36 commented that they were usually beside the road to a place of worship and pilgrimage, or sometimes on the road to the cemetery or a monastery. Informants 23 and 26 said that such trees grew where a saint was buried or a holy man had lived, but Informant 41 said that this belief was perpetuated only by women. Informant 43, from Van, described a holy tree in his area. It was dried up, but it had many different colored rags tied to its branches. People believed that leaving some part of their garments on this tree would bring them the answer to their prayers; sometimes the rags were left by people who sought cures for illnesses. "Let my illness stay behind," they said.[10]

Holy trees were, of course, beneficial, but the walnut tree was popularly supposed to have an evil effect. Walnut trees were believed to contain "electricity," whereby a person's image could be registered on the bark. If this happened, he would surely die. Accordingly, only individuals who had already lived a long time were allowed to plant walnut trees.

The Armenians revered certain white animals: bulls, horses, mules, and rams. They had a taboo on eating the flesh of the horse, mule, ass, dog, cat, mouse, frog, snake, and lizard, and they would not kill certain birds of spring: the stork, crane, dove, nightingale, and starling.[11]

The most interesting and extensive set of beliefs about animals reported by the Detroit informants, however, were those associated with snakes, and especially so-called saint snakes. If a snake took up residence in or near an Armenian dwelling, the family welcomed it, regarding it as a protector of family property, and fed it milk.[12] (Snakes helped, of course, to destroy rodents that could get at the grain stored in the maran.) Informant 47 said that a snake killed in the house would become an enemy and bring misfortune to the household. Informant 25 remarked that saint snakes liked to live near the toneer, but Informant 5 said that they lived in the dirt of the dahneek. Families sometimes put the image of a snake on the pillars, doors, and goods of the house or carved a stone image of a snake at a nearby spring. Pregnant women also sometimes wore snake-shaped amulets.[13]

Informant 47 told two stories which indicate the importance of snakes in Armenian belief.

> In Terses, there was a great well where the world's snakes lived. They were very big and thick, and it was believed that if they came up to the earth, they could ruin it and everyone on it. Every day, therefore, every man in the town threw a liver down to the snakes so that they would be satisfied and not seek further food on the earth.

> A man went into his garden and saw a big snake climbing a tree, intending to eat some little birds in their nest. [This is a common motif in Armenian folktales.] The man said, "Come down, or I will hit you." The snake paid no attention to him. The man repeated his request three times, and each time the snake ignored him. In order to harm it, the man had to repeat a prayer designed especially for snakes. This prayer was so powerful that snakes could not escape their doom. As the man started the special prayer, the snake began

to feel the effect and clung closely to the tree. But finally it could not resist any longer. It fell off the tree and the man threw a stone and killed it.

Comparisons

Many peoples in eastern Europe and the Near East shared with the Armenians a reverence for the same "special" parts of nature. They revered Mother Earth, certain stones, certain springs, and believed in water nymphs.[14] Many also considered Friday a holy day, associated with pure water and the female. Persian women, like Armenian women, had taboos against working on Wednesday and Friday, especially on doing laundry, for they said that the water on Friday "belonged to Fatima."[15] The ritual of stimulating rainfall by yoking women to a plow was also found in northern India.[16] The Eastern Slavs also believed that the newly dead might bring drought because, given its thirst, the corpse absorbed moisture from the land around it.[17]

Most peasants in eastern Europe and the Near East revered the hearth fire. So did the ancient Greeks and Romans.[18] Other Caucasian peoples revered the peaks of high mountains. In Minoan Crete (second millennium B.C.) sanctuaries in caves near mountain peaks also were common, and were associated with summer grazing at higher altitudes.[19] The practice of tying a piece of cloth to a holy tree to make a wish come true was widespread in eastern Europe and the Near East and extended also to India and the British Isles.[20] Another very widespread peasant custom in eastern Europe and the Near East was to adopt a house snake and feed it in the belief that it helped the family.[21]

Saints' Legends

Most of the great churches in Armenia possessed some relic of the saints for whom they were named. For example, the wrist of the patron saint hung on the wall of Saint Toros Church; in it resided the power of the church. The cross was the source of power in Saint Gregory's Church, and in Kana Gudur, it was in the saint's breast. Villagers, however, rarely—if ever—had the opportunity to visit such great churches. Nevertheless, Christianity was an important part of everyday life, and the Detroit informants recalled a variety of legends and personal experiences from their own native villages.

Several legends were told about the miraculous church called Akor Bab, in the tiny village of Akor in Kharpert province. Informant 16 heard the following story from her husband.

> One day a shepherd attended a service at Akor Bab and, to his amazement, saw that each person in the congregation carried a saddle on his back. The priest carried two. The shepherd said to himself, "Perhaps this is the custom now. Let me quickly get one for myself." So he returned to his animals, fetched a saddle, and carried it over his shoulder to the church.
>
> When the people saw the strange sight, they began to laugh at the simple shepherd. The priest asked him why he was wearing a saddle, and the shepherd replied, "As I look around, I see that each person has a saddle on his back. And you, just look at you—you have two!"
>
> The priest, a wise man, said to his flock, "My people, don't laugh at this man. He is the innocent among us. He is wearing a real saddle that we all can see and make fun of. But what we can't see are the sins and wrongdoings that we carry on our own shoulders. Only the innocent among us has the power to see them."

Informant 13, from Akor itself, recalled that Akor Bab was renowned throughout the vicinity as a source for miraculous cures. Those afflicted with paralysis, in particular, made pilgrimages there and were always cured. Turks and Kurds prayed and lit candles there as well as Christians. As a matter of fact, it was just such an infidel who, upon having his prayers answered, left his candles still burning when he departed. As a result, a great fire occurred and the church could be used again only after extensive reconstruction. Unfortunately, it had lost some of its power.

Other churches in the Kharpert area were also the scenes of miraculous cures. Informant 16 mentioned Saint Varvara Church in Hussenig, which was famous for relieving maladies of the eye; a church at Asdvazemehr, between Kharpert and Hussenig, was sought out by epileptics, according to Informant 13. This informant said that there was a small cradle at the back of the church. If the cradle moved when the sick person touched it with a blue bead, the cure would be granted; otherwise, it would not.

Miraculous happenings were possible at places other than churches. Informant 26, from Hakusdun, in the mountains near Kughee, told an interesting anecdote about some caves near the local church. These caves were occupied by holy men who spent their lives in prayer. They lived on one *nshkhark* ("holy wafer") a day. When a new church was to be built, the cave people were told to go away. Once they had left the village behind, they looked back and cursed it: "Neither flourish nor diminish; neither ascent nor descent." And that is how it happened. There were sixty households in Hakusdun then, and the number remained the same.

Informant 16 supplied many details about a striking rock formation near Hussenig that was particularly associated with Saint Sarkis. Two huge, high rocks formed a natural arch; on the rocks, close to the ground, there were many hoofprints. It was commonly believed that Saint Sarkis had ridden over the rocks and left the prints. The spot was supposed to be magical, therefore. Sick babies were taken there to be cured, and young girls often went to the rocks to ask the saint if they would soon marry or if they would get good husbands. Each girl picked up a small stone and placed it among the Saint Sarkis rocks. If the two rocks stuck together, the girl's wish would come true.

Other sources confirm that Saint Sarkis was particularly identified with romantic love. He shaped the destiny of young lovers, and was the functional equivalent of Saint Valentine, the ancient Greek god Eros, and the ancient Armenian god, Ara the Beautiful. On January 21, his feast day, youths ate salty bread, hoping to dream that their future spouse would come with water and satisfy their longings. They put out food for birds so that they could guess, from the direction in which the birds carried it, the place where they would find their future mate. In Nor Nakhichevan girls would gather at the house of an engaged girl and gossip. Young men could not come in, but might surround the house and eaves-drop. Girls might fast for five days in the hope of having good weather on their wedding days.[22]

A dish customarily cooked for Saint Sarkis Day was *pokhint*, a delicacy made of flour and butter, sweetened with honey. Accord-ing to tradition, when the saint was fighting the Georgians, the fried wheat in his pocket turned into pokhint. Armenians put some of the pokhint outside the front door as an offering for him. They also believed that Saint Sarkis protected them from storms, espe-cially when they were traveling. According to legend, the saint, having kidnapped a Byzantine girl, rushed away on horseback from west to east, raising a storm of snow and dust on a road without snow.[23]

Informant 13 knew of the exploits identified with the holy man called Nadre Baba. At night, Nadre Baba slipped out of the small house that enclosed his burial plot and traveled around. Good people could see the illumination surrounding him, but sinners could not. Sick persons who went to his little building and prayed sincerely were cured. The Turks, however, felt that his influence was too great, so they closed the building and put a guard over it to keep believers away. One evening the guard urinated under the window. Immediately his mouth twisted to the back of his head and he could not speak; his arms and legs also became paralyzed. Government officials were notified of his experience, and although they did not believe in the saint's power, they helped to circulate the story and placed a person to collect an entrance fee from those who came to be cured.

Nadre Baba's tomb inside the building faced the east. The Turks turned it around so that it would face the opposite direction, but every time they did so, by morning it had righted itself and was facing east again.

Seasonal Celebrations

Ritual observances in rural Armenia, as in other Christian coun-tries, basically were tied to the major church holidays. These, of course, ultimately were seasonal celebrations as well. Villagers had their biggest celebrations before Lent, around Easter (after finishing their sowing), and in the summer, before harvest. Since they frequently celebrated weddings in the fall, they had no major seasonal rituals at that time.

There were no uniform and widespread rituals on January 1 in Armenia. (Some scholars believe that the Armenians originally did not celebrate the New Year on this day.) Lisitsian reports that on New Year's Eve Armenians poured liquor on the grave monuments of those who had died in the past year, and that a godfather would receive gifts from the families for whom, in the past year, he had christened a child, and from newlyweds at whose wedding he had officiated.[24]

Bdoyan says that only Armenians in southern Armenia and parts of Khorin Haik observed January 1 seriously. They would try to put an end to all quarrels before New Year's Eve. On New Year's Day, men bearing brandy and fruits visited friends, the village headman, and the priest. Women and grooms-to-be visited brides-to-be. Fiancés exchanged apples. The dahn deegeen would decorate the doors of the home with crosses and red threads, while others put up red clothing on the outside as decoration. The male and female household heads passed out fruit and preserves to family members. In some localities housewives made bread in special shapes, representing human figures and animals and the twelve-month round of the year. They might pour wheat into water to get plenty of rain in the coming year.

Bdoyan also reports that the New Year was a time of concern for tools. In some places old women drew pictures of their work tools on the outer wall of the house, and the image of the plowshare on the front door. This was also a time for "threatening" fruit trees and grape vines that had borne little or no fruit. Wielding an ax, their owner would pretend he was about to cut down the barren plant, hoping to scare it into productivity in the coming year.[25]

Informant 16, from Kharpert, was the only one of the Detroit group to describe any observance connected with January 1. She spoke of *gaghantel-ing*, "Christmas gifting," the neighborhood spring from which the family collected water the year around. The mother and children, carrying gifts of nuts and dried fruits, visited the fountain early on New Year's Day, offering prayers of thanksgiving for the events of the past year and asking for good fortune in the year to come. They then collected a jug of water and returned home, leaving the gifts behind. Often the water froze before they reached their destination, and many fantasized that this water would magically turn to gold.

Like some Orthodox Christians, Armenian villagers celebrated Christmas on January 6. The Armenian Christmas is known as *Gaghant* and the Armenian Santa Claus is an invisible spirit called Gaghant Baba ("Father Christmas"). Like other church holidays, Christmas was preceded by a fast. On that day the village priest might lower a cross into the local river, whose water was magical for the time. This was also a day for liberating doves.[26]

On Christmas Day, the children, having tied an empty stocking or sack on a rope, went from roof to roof throughout the village, lowering the rope through the yertik at each house. The people below filled the stocking with nuts and raisins and passed it up again. Meanwhile, the father, knowing that his children needed new shoes or clothing, had delayed his purchases until Christmas, so that the children could say, "Gaghant Baba brought them to us." In some places, according to Informant 16, children went from house to house, singing "Gaghant Baba has come; he has brought us shoes, shoes, shoes" (or whatever clothing had been purchased). The household stayed awake all night, sharing treats with visitors.

An occasion called *Diarendas* (an altered form of *Tyarnendaraj,* "the going ahead of Christ") was celebrated sometime between Christmas and the beginning of Lent. The traditional date seems to have been February 14, but the Detroit informants recalled several different dates. Because this was a day for ritual bonfires, some scholars think that it was originally dedicated to the fire and sun god, Mihr (cf. Mithra). The pagan Armenians called February "the month of Mihr." In any case, in its typical form the ceremony contains obvious reminiscences of fertility rites.

A huge community bonfire was the focal point of Diarendas. Apparently it usually was kindled in the churchyard after services, although Informant 5, from Kharzeet, spoke of it as being on the roof of the gom, and Informant 2, from Fenesé, said that it was "right outside the house." The primary celebrants in most villages were those who had recently married, both male and female, but others also participated. Avedis Aharonian describes the ceremony in considerable detail.

> Each year, on the 13th of February, after the Vesper service, a big brazier is lighted in the courtyard of the church. All the village gathers around it. In the first ranks are placed the newly married couples of that year, holding candles which they have lighted from the sacred fire. They turn three times around the brazier as the flames have the virtue of fertilizing their union, and of giving to their descendants happiness and health. Then come the mothers, holding their babes in their arms. They perform the same round to preserve their children from evil spirits and sickness, while the sterile brides burn the edges of their head-covers to bring fecundity upon them. Others jump over the brazier to become purified. All the assistants mingle their shouts of mirth with the crackling of the flames. After a while the crowd gathers, each returns to his home, holding the candle in his hand to continue the glorification of the fire in his own family. On the roofs braziers are lighted with the candles brought from the church and the same rites are repeated around the family hearth. From every side the shots of guns are heard.
>
> In the houses where there are newly married couples, this festival has a particular importance and solemnity. The parents and friends, laden with presents, come to this home to share the ceremony with them, which they call "taking the young bride to the roof." There the bridegroom kindles the fire with his candle, and while the flames rise, the musicians play a nuptial march. The young couple make the round of the fire three times. As at the time of the marriage festival, they drink to the health of the new hearth. The patriarch of the house predicts, from the direction of the smoke, the side of the field that will be most fertile, while the grandmother takes a handful of ashes and throws it into the stables to preserve the cattle from sickness and to make favorable the laying of eggs. Others throw

ashes behind their shoulders while pronouncing the sacred formula
for "the butter to be abundant." This Fire Festival has the virtue of
healing cureless maladies; that is the reason why sick people are
taken to the roof by means of a rope.[27]

Information from the Detroit group corroborates many of the
details of this account, and several of the informants added some
minor variations. Informant 28, from Palou, Kharpert region, said
that when the evening came to a close, everyone took home a
piece of the burnt wood, believing that it would bring them luck.
Informant 5, from Kharzeet, on the other hand, said that each
person took a piece of the still burning wood for a torch and visited
the graves of his relatives.

Of all of the Armenian observances, however, those connected
with Easter were and remain the most important. For example,
Pareegentahn, the Armenian equivalent of Mardi Gras, was observed just before the start of Lent. Often friends ate together,
feasting on rich food and katah. Any leftovers were thrown out,
because such food could not be kept in the house during Lent.

This pre-Lenten period was a time of betrothals and weddings.
It was also a time of humorous role reversals between monks and
novices, rich and poor, young and old, as license briefly was given
to the underdog to mock his or her betters. This occasion was a
safety valve for hostilities; in the long run it served to establish the
social hierarchy more securely. There were masquerades, proces-
sions, games, and plays. The Armenians also engaged in ritual
swinging at this time; girls sat on swings and boys pushed them. In
the Van basin, the dahn deegeen, having taken her daughter in her
arms, or else a heavy stone mortar, would sit on a swing and be
pushed in order to obtain the equivalent weight in butter in the
coming year.[28]

Armenians observed Lent very strictly, with the entire family
abstaining from butter, cheese, milk, eggs, and meat. Special kinds
of food were prepared. Frequently parents stuck seven feathers
into an onion (Informant 37) or an orange (Informant 15) at the
start of Lent, removing one feather weekly until the Lenten period

was over. As this occurred, children knew that they were one week closer to Easter.

According to Bdoyan, in some parts of Armenia the feathers were inserted in an onion which formed the single foot of an old-man figure called "Aklatiz" or "Akhloj." According to tradition, on the last day of Lent he became a bird and flew away, with the option to return the next year. Did he represent the spirits of the dead, whom the Armenians honored on Merelotz?

These sources also report that on the first day of Lent in the Hark region, each housewife made stars out of dough and put them on the blackened ceiling of the toneer room to form a map of the sky. On the columns of the house she portrayed animals in dough. In some villages, on Good Friday the blacksmith made iron amulets to protect children from lightning and nightmares. A bride-to-be sent her fiancé an embroidered egg to hang on the wall as protection against evil spells.[29]

Easter was the greatest Armenian church holiday, marked by feasting and visiting. Some villages sacrificed a bull and had a communal meal. Eggs were boiled in water with onion skins until they were dyed a deep reddish brown, and individual egg fights were the custom of the day. Antagonists tapped the tips of their eggs together to see which one cracked. The owner of the tough egg captured the cracked one. Informant 3, from Karaghil, knew of a custom whereby the church deacons exchanged red eggs with each other on Easter Day, making them *khach yeghpayrner* ("god-brothers"). When a man and woman made this exchange, they became *khach yeghpayr* and *khach kuyr* ("god-brother" and "god-sister") and could not marry.

On the day after Easter, the villagers took food and drink to the cemetery. After praying over the dead, some informants said, they sat among the graves and ate a meal. However, others said that the food was left on the graves and the poor people of the area came to take it away. Sometime during the week, the local priest visited the homes of his parishioners and made special prayers for their good health.[30]

Some minor rituals occurred on fixed days in spring. April 7 was

Lady Day, the Annunciation of the Virgin. A barren woman might make a pilgrimage to a holy mountain peak to ask for a child. In the Van region people brought earth from the fields to church for blessing and then ran back to the fields and replaced it. On May 6 and 7 the Armenians practised divination concerning the crop yields of the coming year.[31]

On the fortieth day after Easter (usually in May) the Armenians celebrated Ascension Day, which they called Hampartzoum. This holiday, resembling the English May Day, was a time for women's rituals. Hampartzoum fell on a Friday, which, as noted above, was a day associated with female supernatural beings in eastern Europe and the Near East. According to Informant 5, on Ascension Day the village girls collected water from seven streams in a jar beautifully decorated with flowers; each girl then placed some object in the jar. While a song about *veejag* ("fortune") was sung, a child put her hand into the jar and removed an object. The girl who had placed it in the jar would experience the luck mentioned at that moment in the song.

Informant 16, from Kharpert, provided a detailed description of another version of this ceremony. The young girls of her village called the fortieth day after Easter Veejag. They made a large clay container resembling a girl, which they then dressed with bright clothing and a veil. Then the girls went to the mountain and gathered some of all of the different flowers growing there. They went to seven brooks and took a cup of water from each. Then they put the water and the flowers into the girl-shaped container, along with a personal possession such as a ring or a pin of each of the girls. (Some said that the vessel must be hidden in full moonlight for a time because the stars which shone on it determined destiny.) Accompanied by a little girl and the priest's wife, nicely dressed with colorful handkerchieves and a long veil, the girls went from house to house, visiting everyone. As they moved along, they sang:

> Luck has come, has come to our door.
> She has a dress of handkerchieves and a veil on her face.
> I will steal stone, and from seven brooks, I will steal water;
> The flowers from their stems I will steal.

Today is Hampartzoum!
If you ask the girls [to marry you], the world will become topsy-
turvy
[that is, one must ask the parents; otherwise, the world would be
in great confusion].

People gave them good things to eat, or, more often, flour and
butter. These things were taken to a specified place where the
adults gathered.

After visiting all the households in the village, they went to the
priest's house. When all the girls were assembled, the priest's wife
said, "Luck, luck, open; the flowers are open." Then the little girl
put her hand in the container and brought up the first token, while
the maidens gathered around to see to whom it belonged and what
the priest's wife would prophesy about the future of the owner.
Then the group went to the place where the food had been sent,
joining everyone from the village. There was dancing and eating.

Informants 3, 5, and 46 recalled that their native villages celebrated a variation of the spring festival in which young men played
a larger role. After decorating a wooden pole or "tree" with
flowers and a bell, they carried it from door to door, asking for
butter, eggs, and flour. Then they went up into the mountains and
had a picnic. Sometimes they were accompanied by *davoul* and
zourna, drum and fifelike instruments. The published sources,
however, indicate that in other areas the young men chose the one
among them they thought most handsome to play "groom," adorn-
ing him with multicolored scarves and little bells. These youths
also collected food around the village, finally joining the girls for a
picnic.[32]

The ritual of *Vartavar* occurred ninety-eight days after Easter,
and usually fell in July. According to Melik-Pashayan, *vart* in Hit-
tite means "water sprinkling." In Armenian it means "rose." In
July the Armenians were usually in the high pastures with their
flocks, and it was customary for people to sprinkle each other with
water and dunk each other in streams. In some places they released white doves. It was supposed to be lucky for a girl and
youth to meet for the first time on this day. In the Dersim region,

the people sacrificed any calves with a white star or a white half-moon on the brow to the pagan goddess Anahit on this day. They believed such calves were fathered by bulls of Anahit which lived in the mountains.[33]

On the Sunday nearest August 15 came the Assumption of the Virgin and the blessing of the first fruits of the year's harvest in church.

Some scholars think that the pagan Armenians began the New Year on or near August 6. According to Bdoyan, around the turn of the century the Armenians in Persia and in the Sıunik, Artsakh, and Gandzak regions celebrated the New Year during August 1–6 by outdoor banquets featuring the ritual dish hereseh.[34] Benik E. Tumanian has suggested that this celebration coincided with the heliacal rising of the constellation Orion, whom the Armenians identified with Haig, their eponymous hero.[35] There is also circumstantial evidence in support of this hypothesis. It was logical for the ancient Armenians to begin the new year in early August because this was the beginning of the crop year, the time to begin harvesting most of the plant foods they would have to depend upon until the next August. The weather in August was excellent for outdoor celebration, in contrast to the severe cold of January 1. Moreover, female personages, (Anahit, and later the Virgin Mary) were associated with this holiday, and in pre-Christian religions a female personage was often dominant.

Comparisons

Orthodox Christians in eastern Europe and the Near East also observed January 6, which they regarded as Epiphany, not Christmas. Like the Armenians, they dipped the cross into river or lake water on this day.

The Greeks also tried to predict when and whom they would marry by eating salty bread. They did this either on Saint Catherine's Day (November 26) or on the first day of Lent.[36]

Bonfire rituals similar to Diarendas were found in many parts of Europe, but they usually occurred at the solstices. The timing of this ritual among the Armenians was most likely influenced by Zoroastrianism. The Azeris, who were formerly Zoroastrians, had a similar ritual on February 21.[37]

The period just before Lent—variously known as Shrovetide, Carnival, Fastnacht, Mardi Gras, and Maslenitsa, was a time of masquerades, role reversals, and merrymaking thoughout Europe and the Christian communities in the Near East. In Lithuania the peasants enjoyed ritual swinging at this time.[38] Elsewhere such swinging occurred around Easter or at the solstices. A Lenten seven-week "calendar" made of onion and feathers was found also among the Greeks of the Pontus provinces (northern Anatolia). The Palestinian Christian Arabs believed that during Lent the souls of the dead came to visit the living.[39]

The Armenian Hampartzoum ritual of divination with a jar was similar to the Greek Kledonas ceremony, held on June 24, which involved drawing tokens from a jar of water exposed overnight to the stars.[40] The sprinkling of water was also practiced by the Persians around July 25.[41]

Both the Greeks and Slavs celebrated August 6 and associated it with the Virgin and the blessing of first fruits. There are indications that the Greeks, too, once considered early August the beginning of the new year.[42]

In summary, one may say that Armenians in rural areas at the turn of the century, although practicing Christians, also retained many pagan attitudes and customs. They revered certain aspects of nature, especially fertile soil, pure spring water, and the hearth fire. They observed changes in the season with rituals which while Christianized, contained reminiscences of pagan rites. In their attitudes toward "special" parts of nature, the Armenians resembled many other peoples of Europe and the Near East. Their veneration of springs and mountain peaks was typical of peoples of the semiarid alpine areas of eastern Anatolia and the Caucasus. Some Armenian seasonal rituals, notably the pre-Lent and the post-Easter festivities, resembled those of Eastern Orthodox Christians, especially the Greeks.

Omens

Armenians believed in destiny, *jagadakeer,* which literally means
"what is written on the forehead." One had to accept misfortune
stoically because it was unavoidable. However, their strong belief
in predestination was accompanied by an equally strong desire to
discover what the future would bring before it actually came to
pass, either through divination or by interpreting the hidden meaning of dreams or of everyday occurrences. For example, Informant
47, herself a fortune-teller and folk healer, said that there were
children in Erzunga who could tell anyone what he wished to know
about the future. A cloth was thrown over the child's head and he
gazed into a glass of water. This informant also described a girl in
the same village who rubbed her fingernails and then saw in them
images of whatever she sought to interpret or foretell.

Armenians used omens from everyday life to predict the future,
but also to reveal hidden truths about the past and present. The
following are some omens originally collected from Detroit-area
Armenians during World War II that are still current.

If your ears ring, someone is talking about you.

If your left eye twitches, it means bad luck. (These two omens
were also found among the Greeks and Persians.)[43]

If you hiccough persistently, that means you have stolen something.

If you sneeze on either New Year's Eve or New Year's Day, you
are rolling off the old year and accepting the new.

If you look into a mirror at night, you will go crazy. (A similar idea
was found among the Persians and Southern Slavs.)[44]

If you leave a bit of food on your plate, you will marry someone
with a scarred face, but if you lick your plate clean, you will
get a handsome fiancé.

If you jump over the feet of a child as it lies on the floor, you must
jump back or you will stunt its growth.

If you drop a strand of hair on the floor and someone steps on it,
you will get a headache.

If someone who loves you obtains a bit of your hair, he may force
  you to reciprocate his love. (A similar idea was found in Persia
  and among the Uzbeks.)[45]
If you say something bad at the table, God will punish you and
  take away the food. It is a sin to laugh at the table.
If you start to make a dress and a white witch enters the room, the
  work will be easy.
If a dog howls, a member of your family will soon die. The remedy
  is to turn the slippers of the person whom you think may be in
  danger upside-down. (This belief was also found in Persia.)[46]
If you eat burned bread, you will be brave and bears will not
  attack you.
If you steal money, candles, or anything else from a church, you
  will become paralyzed and dumb.

Similarly, dreams might foretell the future. When someone an-
nounced that he had had a dream, it was customary to say, "may it
be good," in order to forestall bad luck.

The following images in dreams were good omens:

horse	church
fish	clock
bread	drinking or bathing in
wine	clear water
long hair	playing
reading, writing	silver coins or paper money
lighted room	

The following images were bad omens:

camel	new shoes
ox	electric shock
cow	drinking or bathing in
donkey	dirty water
snake	cutting hair
dog	dancing
lion	your house in poor condition

Other omens:

a cat running after you = you have eaten something and failed to
    share it. The person you neglected has become the cat.

mouse = trouble, because something you have said about someone
    else reached the ear of that person

dove = innocence

chicken, egg = gossip

removing a shoe = getting out of trouble

attending a wedding = someone will die in the family you visited

mulberries or excretion = you will receive money

yourself in weeds = you will have a hard time

ring on your finger = you will be unhappy, but if it is a silver ring,
    you will be happy

visiting and eating with a family = you will receive a gift from an
    unexpected place

kissing the hand or face of the dead = you will receive news from a
    place far away

a drunken man = you will receive bad news from a dear friend

man who appears dead but is really alive = he will live longer

a sick person getting better = he will die instead

painting your house white = death to some member of the family

singing = you will hear of something, good or bad

putting out the flame of a lamp = some misfortune will come to
    the people in the house

soapy hair = grief, but if rinsed well = happiness

climbing a hill = you will get rid of your trouble, but if you try to
    climb and cannot = you are in great trouble

7.

FOLK MEDICINE, ILLNESS, AND DEATH

University-trained doctors did not practice in the Armenian villages. Such physicians did occasionally visit rural communities, but it was certainly possible for a villager to be born, live a long life, and die without ever having been seen by one. The villagers had local midwives to help at childbirth and individuals who were skilled at setting bones and dealing with accidental injuries or other emergencies, but fundamentally they relied upon a store of remedies passed down over the generations. Unfortunately, there still are few formal studies of folk medicine or of the customary ways of coping with death among Near Eastern peoples.[1]

Rural Armenians believed that illness might come from four possible sources: (1) the influence of a living person, often described as that of "the evil eye"; 2) an evil spirit, such as an al; 3) a dead person, especially a recently dead person who wished to take someone else to the other world; or 4) a saint, angered by someone who did violence to his or her remains or holy shrines.[2] The germ theory of disease was still generally unknown in Armenian villages at the turn of the century. Nevertheless, in many cases Armenian folk healers, using their traditional methods, probably did more good than harm.

The Evil Eye

Armenian beliefs and practices connected with the evil eye are particularly interesting. Like all their neighbors in the Near East, and many others in Europe and Africa, Armenians believed that one living person could harm another by looking at and envying his property or person. Moreover, the power was not to be taken lightly. According to Informant 48, it could make a stone burst and an animal die in the field. In the Near East this belief was probably older than Judaism, Christianity, or Islam.

In a recent comparative study of various cultures, John M. Roberts identified some variables correlated with belief in the evil eye. All of these traits were characteristic of Armenian culture at the turn of the century: 1) animal husbandry, especially milking and dairying activity; 2) cereal cultivation and use of the plow; 3) mining, quarrying, smelting, and metalworking; 4) social inequality, an unstable, tax-farming government, and pastoral raiding; 5) patronage and god-kinship; 6) a patrilineal descent system; 7) child-rearing practices which included little father involvment, no encouragement of early motor skills, but early encouragement of modesty and sexual restraint; young boys taught to be industrious, responsible, obedient, but not trusting; 8) belief in a supreme god. However, anthropologists have not yet reached a consensus on an explanation for evil-eye beliefs.[3]

Whatever the underlying causes for belief in the evil eye, the Detroit informants indicated that it was greatly feared. Persons were in particular danger if they were to be envied for some reason or—perhaps also an occasion for envy in a culture which valued children—if they were pregnant. The Armenian villager used a number of preventatives and cures for the evil eye, which also were widespread in the Mediterranean and the Middle East. One of the most popular was wearing something blue, and blue items were especially common on babies' garments. Usually a blue bead or a clove of garlic was attached to the band or hat or on the shoulder of a young child; Informant 2 said that sometimes a blue ribbon was worn under the arm.

Metal objects also were particularly efficacious because, according to Informant 22, metal attracted the "vibrations" from evil spirits and the evil eye, directing them away from human beings. This informant recounted an experience in which a grandmother, in order to protect her grandson's pregnant wife, pointed a knife at the young woman's stomach, mumbled prayers that lasted two minutes, and then moved the knife over the head and between the head and waistline of the expectant mother. Finally, she spit on the knife and stuck it in the wood molding next to the floor with instructions not to remove it for at least a week. In this same household, a horseshoe decorated with blue stones was above the door. The opening of the horseshoe was toward the ground. Like the knife, it would direct evil influences away from family members. A variant of this belief in metal held that one could break an evil-eye spell affecting a baby by striking a nail on the ground under its cradle (Informant 26).

A visitor to a household avoided praising a child so as not to be suspected of envy and hence of wishing to do harm. This was particularly true of those unusual Armenians who had red hair and blue or gray eyes, since such people were thought to be likely to cause damage. A visitor who did say nice things about a child would first say, "God keep him [or her] in good health." Then, according to Informant 48, the parent would say something bad about the child so as to counteract the evil eye.[4] Older children were warned to scratch their buttocks as a means of self-protection if they were admired. Individuals who thought they were envied put a piece of burning coal or wood into water and said, "God protect us from the evil eye."[5]

Weariness and yawning, mild symptoms of the effect of the evil eye, could be cured by a healer who followed certain procedures (Informants 4, 47). She might take salt in her palm, rubbing some of it on the forehead and putting some of it into the mouth of the sufferer, praying as she did so. If the healer yawned, she had broken the spell; if the afflicted one felt better, the cure was considered to be effective. The healer would then sprinkle salt here and there in the village so that people walked on it. Sometimes salt was dropped on the doorstep of the person who allegedly gave the evil eye, thereby giving back to that person the physical illness the afflicted person was experiencing.[6]

These formulas and precautions suggest that the Armenians feared and distrusted their neighbors, notwithstanding their mutual need for security and approval. In a sense, they were caught in a dilemma: if they failed to achieve, this brought them public shame; if they achieved too much, this brought public envy.

Healing

Detroit informants told of a number of remedies that families and folk healers used for common complaints. They mentioned no remedies for such serious conditions as malaria, typhoid, typhus, and smallpox.[7] It is interesting, however, that informants reported a general belief that both syphilis and smallpox had been introduced into Armenia by the Turkish army, in order to make the Armenian men waste away and lose their strength. They called syphilis *Frankee aghd* ("French dirt"). The only cure mentioned, by Informant 15, was to starve the infected person for forty days.

Almost all folk healers around the world recommend bleeding for certain conditions, and the Armenian healers were no exception.[8] They used bleeding mainly for localized bodily pain and swelling. The healer (either an older woman of the family or the village barber) began by cupping the sore spot with the horn of a small goat. She ignited a piece of paper and dropped it into the horn, which was quickly affixed to the skin of the patient, when the heat dissipated, she removed the horn and used a razor to make scratches on the raised circle. After the blood had flowed she splashed rakhee on the spot to keep it clean. (Albanians and Southern Slavs also used rakhee in this way.)[9] Or, instead of a razor, she might put leeches to suck on the cupped area (Informants 16, 47). After they had had their fill, she placed them on salt until they had vomited the blood. The healer then squeezed them to extract the last drops of blood and returned them to a jar of clean water to await their next use.

Other common procedures mentioned by Informants 2, 16, 27, and 47 were the following:

Anemia: Feed the patient a mixture of butter and honey.
Baldness: Grind the flower called *degd;* mix it with just enough water to make a soft paste. Apply it to the bald spot.

Boils: Mix an egg yolk with salt and spread it on an unwashed cloth. Place this on the boil.

Broken bones: Use a tree branch stripped of its bark for a splint. Bring the broken pieces together, tie them into place, and massage the area. Make a mixture of figs and fat from the tail of the broadtail sheep, place it in a cloth, and bind it on the break. The next day, replace the first mixture with one made of black raisins and ground black pepper. Leave this mixture in place for several days.

To help a broken leg set quickly, salt an egg yolk and mix it with unwashed wool. Spread the mixture in an unwashed cloth and wrap it around the leg.

Burns: Boil a mixture of butter, olive oil, and beeswax. Allow it to cool, and then apply it to the burn, using a hen's feather.

Boil a mixture of lime and water. Strain the liquid and return it to boiling. Repeat this process seven times. Apply the liquid to the burn with a hen's feather.

Place madzoon in a bag, allowing it to drain until only the curd remains. Apply the curd to the burn.

Chest colds: Crumble a dried hollyhock flower and boil it with water into a tea for the patient to drink.

Coughing: Feed the patient a quince filled with incense and then roasted.

Cysts: Melt lead and bind it on the swelling.

Dysentery: Feed the patient unwashed rice.

Eye diseases: Blindfold the patient and lead him to where the weed called *hohdehd* grows. Cut the root from the plant and collect the milky sap. Put the sap in the patient's eye.

Headache: Apply henna to the patient's head. (Many of the older Armenian women in the Delray community of Detroit continued to use this cure. It thus was not unusual to see grandmothers with carrot-red hair.)

Obesity: Make the patient wear lead inside his clothing until the flesh melts away.

Shock (fright): Massage the patient's body, starting at the trunk. Repeat as necessary.

Grasp the patient's trunk and exert pressure on both sides of his body. As the pressure is released, the patient will feel a warm, tingling sensation that will gradually spread through his body and relieve the shock.

Have the patient drink some of his own urine.

Have the patient eat an onion, apple, or quince roasted with a piece of incense at the center.

Take a piece about as big as the end of your thumb of the stone called *pangzaier.* Dissolve it in water and have the patient drink the liquid.

Snakebite: Grind some of the weed called *geednekod.* Wash the bitten area with milk and place the weed on it. After an hour, remove it and again wash the area with milk. Repeat this process seven times.

Sores: Place ground geednekod on the area.

Place a mixture of ground weeds and henna on the patient's hands.

Stomachache: Feed the patient peppermint or boiled anise.

Swelling: Apply a mixture of fat and flour to the area.

Teething pain: Rub the child's gums with rakhee.

Urination:[10] To increase scanty urine, boil parsley and water and have the patient drink the liquid.

Too frequent urination is caused by a weak back. Rub an egg white on the patient's back to strengthen it.

Whooping cough: Shave the middle of the patient's head and draw some blood from the area. Hang a necklace of pumpkin seeds around the patient's neck.

To protect other children from the disease, wrap garlic or camphor in blue cloth and hang it around their necks.

Death

Normally, Armenian villagers died at home, with their families around them to ease their passing. In order to permit the "angel of death" to take away the soul, they would open doors from the sick room. While patients were still alive the family might dress them in their burial dress and place their work tools upon them.[11] The ways the household dealt with dying and death reflect, like their attitudes toward nature, a mixture of Christian and pre-Christian beliefs.

They believed, for example, that the soul had extent and weight which increased if its sins were many. According to Informant 16, if it got too heavy, the soul could not cross the single-strand "bridge of hair" to the other world, but fell into the "inextinguishable fire." While the good soul was like a dove, or filled with light, the bad soul was dark as smut.[12] The Armenians also believed that each soul was linked with a star, lucky or unlucky. As the individual's life failed, his star grew dim; at his death, it fell from the sky. According to some published sources, Armenians believed that it took seven days for the newly released soul to fly to heaven. This period was a particularly dangerous time for the living and the dead. The bereaved family did not cook for two to seven days, and male relatives might not shave for seven days.

Another belief was that the dead needed food and drink for some time after burial, because death was a gradual process of extinction, not sudden and complete. Therefore the villagers made offerings of food on recent graves. Moreover, because those who had recently died were believed to be still reluctant to die, the living feared them. Their souls might still be able to visit the head or liver of a living person. The deceased, grieving for his kin, might try to take one away with him, so it was necessary to secure the deceased person firmly in his grave and hide the way home from him. Since the dead also remained attached to their possessions, the family carefully distributed them so that souls would not remain or return.[13]

To prevent evil spirits from dwelling in the dead body, they washed it. Then they wrapped the body in a white, or sometimes blue, shroud or burial clothing. Reasoning was that since a baby was born "in a shirt" (the amniotic sac), so should a dead person be returned to Mother Earth. The eyes of the dead were closed so that they would not know who buried them or be able to find the way home.[14]

The Detroit informants did not speak much about the beliefs underlying death observances, although several of them did provide detailed descriptions of the traditional practices in different areas. All of these accounts have certain general features in common: the bodies were washed, wrapped in linen (or, according to Informant 3, from Karaghil, near Moush, sewn into a shroud) and usually were buried in the local graveyard. Even in the winter, bodies were buried on the death day, or, if it were too late, the following day. In some villages, the corpse was left overnight in the church (Informants 25, 2, 15, 27, 23) or in a room next to it (Informant 24). Within a few days after the interment, the family shared a memorial meal called *hokeh hatz* (literally, "bread for the soul"; more loosely, "meal for the soul") with the rest of the community. It was not uncommon for families to continue for some time to provide the food in memory of the deceased, occasionally for as long as a year after his death (Informant 4). It is also apparent that there once must have been a generally shared taboo against fires for some period following a death, but by the late nineteenth century, the taboo was observed in some villages (Informants 13, 17, 42) and not in others (Informants 2, 4, 23, 34, 38, 46). Informant 15 described an interesting intermediate stage: the family had to have a fire to heat water to wash the corpse, but the wood for that fire was cut in small slivers and any left over was thrown away, as was any of the water that had been warmed over it.

Through these informants' accounts, it is evident that, just as in daily life, ceremonies connected with death were marked by strong distinctions between male and female roles. How these roles were divided, however, varied by location. For example, according to Informant 5, from Kharzeet, Informant 23, from Sepastia, and Informant 25, from Kughee, women were expected to wash the female bodies and men the male bodies. Informant 34, from Severeg, said that the mother-in-law and the sisters-in-law were responsible for preparing a female corpse, while the deacon washed a man. However, Informant 27, from Malatia, and Informant 17, from Kharadigin, said that women washed all bodies; Informant 15, from Zeitoun, and Informant 7, from Efgere, specified that these were "special old women" from outside the household.

Informant 13, from Akor village, added that in his area whoever washed the dead put bread on his lips and closed his eyelids. If his eyes did not close completely, people said, "achkeh yedevneh" ("his eyes remain behind"; that is, "he is interested in taking someone else along with him"). This informant did not specify that the "bread" was a consecrated wafer, but Informants 15, 22, and 42 mentioned the custom. According to Informant 23, mourners sometimes put a bottle of rakhee in the grave with the corpse, and Informant 7 said that in his village of Efgere, it was the custom for one of the male family members to take rakhee to the cemetery; as the bereaved left the cemetery, he offered a drink for a toast, "orereh tzessee" ("may his days be added to yours").

Attendance at the church and gravesite also was determined by sex. Apparently, the actual funeral procession normally was exclusively male (Informant 41, from Karakehoy, near Adana, remarked that a woman was not prohibited, but he had never seen one participate); women either joined the group at the cemetery (Informant 38) or went the following day (Informants 3, 4, 25, 34). Public lamentation by women, however, was common; Informant 12, from Kessab, knew that at one time professional mourners had been hired, but this was no longer true. Informant 7, however, said that in his village the household women were not even allowed at the cemetery because "they made too much noise," and Informant 42 recalled that while women attended the church ceremony, they did not go to the cemetery.

None of the Detroit informants gave a very complete description of his local cemetery, but some of the published nineteenth-century accounts suggest that the typical grave was a loosely piled mound of earth held down by one or more flat stones. Normally these stones were not inscribed in any way, although Ramsey reports that both the Christian Armenians and Muslims sometimes used ancient carved stones turned up in excavations.[15] Villagers did not usually bury the dead in coffins because wood was too scarce. Instead they might use a wooden litter or a single coffin, which was returned to the village, to carry the dead to the cemetery.

The Monday after each great church holiday was recognized as a memorial day. The most important of these was the observance on the Monday after Easter. The local priest blessed the graves, with whole families in attendance. Although there is some discrepancy as to whether Armenians actually ate a meal at the cemetery at the gravesites of their loved ones at Merelotz, it is true that food was taken there in most localities. Informant 34 said that the priest accompanied the people to the cemetery but no food was taken. Poor people, knowing the custom, were waiting at the entrance of the cemetery for the gifts of food which were given to them. Then the family returned to the deceased's house for a communal meal. In the Caesarea area, said Informant 7, people took *paklava,* a sweet pastry, to the cemetery at Merelotz. After the religious ceremonies, they ate what they wanted and left the rest to the priest. He added, "the priest took much paklava home that day." According to Informant 23, merchants and artisans brought their products, setting up a bazaar outside of the cemetery. Informant 5 indicated that children rolled eggs in the cemetery the day after Easter; Informant 28 remembered that men using canes jousted on their horses at one end of the cemetery.

In addition to observing Merelotz and the ceremonies accompanying the actual death and interment, Armenian villagers were careful to adhere to certain formulaic phrases in referring to deceased relatives, such as "Asdvadz loosavoreh hokeen" ["may God fill his soul with light"] and "ogormatz hokeen" ["his blessed soul"]. Individual households might hold domestic observances as well. Informant 47, for example, vividly recalled the burning of incense on a small tin every Saturday night; as the smoke issued forth, each member of the family, one by one, inhaled the smoke, crossed himself, and prayed for the peace of the souls of the dead. Nevertheless, although Mardiros Ananikian, in "Armenian Mythology," and Avedis Aharonian, in *The Ancient Beliefs of the Armenians according to Armenian Folklore,* speak of ancestor worship among ancient Armenians, there seems to be little evidence of this in the folklife of the late nineteenth century.

Comparisons

Many other peoples in the area had beliefs about the dead similar to those of the Armenians. The belief that the dead had to cross a "bridge of hair" to get to the other world was found among the Caucasian and Altaic peoples. The Eastern Slavs also equated the good soul with a dove. The ancient Romans might put the remains of their dead in a *columbarium* (dove house). The notion that each soul was linked with a star and shared its fortunes was found in eastern Europe, Italy, and India. Even more widespread was the idea that the dead were hungry and thirsty for a period after burial.[16]

Ambivalent feelings toward the dead—grief and fear—were very common. So was the idea that the dead person was reluctant to leave this world and that he might try to come back to take a dear one away.[17]

A funeral shroud, or winding sheet, was typical in many areas of eastern Europe and the Near East. So was the funeral feast immediately after the interment, and the periodic memorial feasts during the following year. The Eastern Slavs, Greeks, and Persians had a memorial feast on the fortieth day. The Persians also observed the seventh day.[18]

Eastern Christians also had a certain day in late spring when all families took food to the graves of their dead. The Russians did this on the Tuesday after Easter (Radunitsa). The Greeks did the same on Rousalia, the forty-ninth day after Easter, a Saturday. The Persians did it sometime in May on Tirdjian. The Palestinians did it a week before Good Friday, either on a Thursday or Friday, or on Maundy Thursday, the day before Good Friday.[19]

Persian women, like Armenian women, were not present at the interment of the dead. Georgian women washed the female dead and Georgian men the male.[20] These customs were not characteristic of eastern European Christians, however.

PUBLISHER'S AFTERWORD

The traditional rural Armenian way of life included strategies for coping with difficult problems. To extract enough food and fuel for themselves from a hard environment, they ate little meat and used wood sparingly. To protect themselves from the raids and extortions of non-Armenians, they lived close to their kinfolk, huddling in naturally fortified villages. Finally, although they could do little to help serious illness, they could ease the pain of death with rituals.

There were both benefits and costs in being Armenian. The benefits were the firm support of family and friends in time of need, and the pleasures of good food, singing, dancing, and socializing on festive occcasions. The good Armenian boy was encouraged to achieve and often did. The good Armenian girl could look forward to a position of authority in her household in middle age.

The costs of being Armenian included the strain of suppressing and hiding feelings of pride, anger, and envy. To be constantly wary, lest one be deceived, was also a strain. Armenians were expected to obey their parents in the choice of work and spouse, as well as to suppress all sexual impulses other than those felt toward the spouse. Christian teachings reinforced these traditional restraints, but the rewards of religion also made the restraints more tolerable.

The villager's way of life also included beliefs and practices that owed nothing to Christianity, but survived because they satisfied needs which Christianity did not satisfy. For example, the Armenians revered certain aspects of nature, especially fertile soil, fresh spring water, and the hearth fire. They revered snow-capped

Mount Ararat and the grape vine, which grew so well on the plain below. The two symbols were complementary: Mount Ararat pointed toward the sky, while the grape vine had deep, thick roots in the earth. Mount Ararat symbolized high aspiration; the grape vine stood for tenacity and abundance. Another symbol, the rosette, probably suggested to the Armenians the eternal renewal of life. Nothing died forever; one could hope.

Although most Armenians may be better off materially now than they were at the turn of the century, they are not necessarily better off culturally. The culture that was developed over many centuries was torn apart and, in some cases, destroyed. Yet those who remember the old way of life have reason to be proud of it. It was an effective strategy for survival, but the Armenians did more than survive. Armenians, within and without their homeland, have become a high-achieving people.

Even prior to the massacres in Turkey, the Armenians were achievers who were able to create their own opportunities. Later, when they settled in numerous host countries in the diaspora and were free to utilize their natural talents and abilities, they succeeded in achieving prominence in every field of endeavor. Some world-famous achievers include Lucine Amara, Charles Aznavour, Lili Chookasian, Calouste Gulbenkian, Victor Hambartsumian, Alan Hovhaness, Yosouf Karsh, Aram Khachaturian, Rouben Mamoulian, Alex Manoogian, Anastas Mikoyan, Set Momjian, William Saroyan, and many more.

Today, in Soviet Armenia, the Armenians enjoy the benefits of modern science and technology. They can tap the mineral and hydroelectric resources of their land. They can obtain scientific medical care. They can study, in their own language, the full range of university-level subjects. They are physically protected by the military power of the Soviet Union.

In most of the western diaspora, Armenians are also physically secure and have access to the advantages of science, technology, and higher education. To be sure, they are more likely to be assimilated into the cultures of their host countries. But they are also freer to explore unconventional ideas and life styles, to travel, and to express unconventional ideas and feelings.

Map of informants' villages

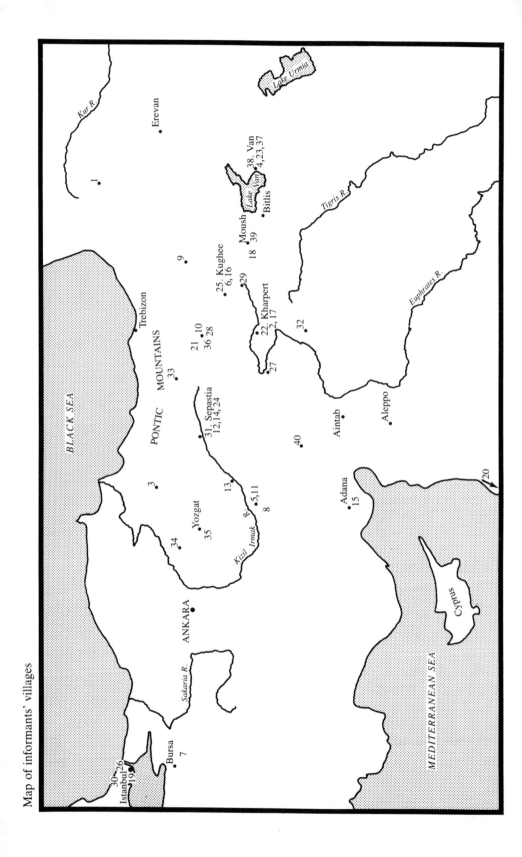

Note: Numbers on map refer to place names on this list.

1. Akhalkalakh
   Informant 37
2. Akor—within Kharpert
   Informant 13
3. Amasia
   Informant 46
4. Aralez—within Van
   Informant 24
5. Caesarea (Kayseri)
   Informant 10
6. Chanakjee—within Kughee
   Informants 29, 38
7. Chengiler
   Informant 23
8. Efgere
   Informant 7
9. Erzeroum
   Informant 11
10. Erzunga
    Informant 1
11. Fenesé—within Caesarea
    Informant 2
12. Gavra—within Sepastia
    Informant 14
13. Ghermehr
    Informant 8
14. Govdun—within Sepastia
    Informant 9

15. Hajin
    Informant 39
16. Hakusdun—within Kughee
    Informant 26
17. Harseg—within Kharpert
    Informant 48
18. Karaghil
    Informant 3
19. Karakehoy—part of Istanbul
    Informant 41
20. Kessab—near Beirut (not on map)
    Informant 12
21. Kharadigin
    Informant 17
22. Kharpert
    Informant 16
23. Kharzeet—within Van
    Informant 5
24. Korsana—within Sepastia
    Informant 18
25. Kughee
    Informants 25, 44
26. Kurdbelem
    Informant 36
27. Malatia
    Informant 27

28. Meghoozeek
    Informant 21
29. Palou
    Informant 28
30. Sabonji (Turkey)
    Informant 20
31. Sepastia
    Informant 22
32. Severeg
    Informant 34, 35
33. Shabinkarahisar
    Informants 30, 31, 32, 33
34. Sohngurlu
    Informant 19
35. Tezeli
    Informant 42
36. Tortan
    Informant 40
37. Urantz—within Van
    Informant 6
38. Van
    Informant 43
39. Vardo-Gundemir—within Moush
    Informants 4, 45
40. Zeitoun
    Informant 15

The home village of Informant 47 is unknown.

BIOGRAPHIES OF INFORMANTS

The informants' biographies are based primarily on materials which Susie Hoogasian Villa collected before her death, and they are necessarily incomplete.

1. Azniv Surmanian Altounian

Born in Erzunga in 1900, daughter of a dry-goods merchant. She attended Armenian parochial school for six years. After living in Trebizond and Istanbul, she came to America in 1918 and married in 1919. She had three daughters and a son and was active in the Armenian church and the Armenian Relief Society.

2. Agavnee Vanarian Alzarian

Born February 14, 1905, in Fenesé, near Caesarea, a town of about fifteen hundred household. Her father, a merchant, died at thirty-one, apparently of appendicitis, and her paternal uncle cared for her and her siblings. During the events of 1915, her uncle took the family on foot to Aleppo, where a French family wanted a servant girl. She stayed there four years before rejoining her family in Damascus. She came to Detroit to marry a businessman from another family in her hometown. They had one living daughter.

3. Mesock Amroian

Born July 6, 1892, in Karaghil, near Moush, a village of two hundred households. Almost half of the inhabitants were members of his clan. He went to an Armenian school for three years, and then studied privately with a well-educated clergyman. His mother died when he was young, and after his father went to America, he was cared for in his paternal gerdastan. When it seemed he would be drafted into the Turkish army, his father arranged for him to come to Detroit, where they were reunited on August 12, 1912. He married twice, losing one wife by death and another by divorce. By the second marriage he had six sons and one daughter.

4. Elmas Artinian

Born around 1895 in the village of Vardo-Gundemir, near Moush. She was the eldest of four children and lost her father young. At thirteen, even though sexually immature, she was married to a youth of about seventeen or eighteen. She had her first child at sixteen. During World War I the men of the household were killed and the women deported. Her young daughter died on the road, but she found refuge with missionaries in Kharpert and then in Aleppo. Somehow her husband escaped with his life and reached Russian Armenia; he sent money for her to join him there. When she and two companions were about to leave, she became very ill and the others left without her. One of them told her husband she had died, and after some time he remarried. Meanwhile, she recovered and wrote to him, but he did not receive her letters. When a relative in America sent her money, she came, married, and had two daughters. Soon afterward, her second husband died in an automobile accident. Eventually she married again, but her third husband died six months later.

5. Levon Asadourian

Born in 1901 in Kharzeet, a village of forty households in the Rushtunian district, Van region. He was the second son among four children. Most of his family were massacred; he escaped to an orphanage in Erevan. His cousin sent him money, and he came to Detroit in 1921. In 1924 he married a girl from his home district, and they had one son and one daughter. In Detroit he worked at the Ford plant.

6. Agavnee Parseghian Asadourian (wife of Informant 5)

Born in 1906 in Urantz, Rushtunian district, Van region. She grew up in a gerdastan. One of her brothers emigrated to the United States. She was nine years old in 1915, when she escaped the massacres and reached Erevan. In 1924 her brother succeeded in bringing her to America, where she married.

7. Karnig Bahadourian

Born in 1894, in Efgere, a town of two thousand inhabitants. His father was a veterinarian and blacksmith. He and his two older brothers were metalworkers, specializing in making knives and scissors. His mother, whose father had started a school for girls, read widely. After graduating from elementary school, he came to Detroit and worked at the Ford plant, married in 1924, and had two children.

8. Maxime Tabibian Bahadourian (wife of Informant 7)

Born in Ghermehr, a village near Caesarea, the youngest of ten children in a prosperous family. When the events of 1915 interrupted her education, she survived with the help of American missionaries, friendly Turks, and her brother, a physician, who served the Turkish government. Another brother sent her money from America, and in 1923 she emigrated with her mother and an older sister. In 1924 she married.

9. Oskee Begian

Born in about 1888 in Govdun, a village of about three hundred to three hundred and fifty households, near Sepastia. She lived in a gerdastan while her father worked as a clerk in Istanbul. She married in 1908 and was pregnant when her husband left for America. During the events of 1915 she was deported and wandered in search of work for five years. Her daughter died. One day two American missionaries told her that her husband in America was trying to find her. She joined him in America about 1918 and had three sons.

10. Heranoush Neffian Dabanian

Born in 1895 in Caesarea in a nuclear family household, one of five children. Her father was a furrier. She attended the Protestant Girls' School in Caesarea until she was sixteen, when she went to the Talas Girls' College for two years. Her future mother-in-law noticed her there and, after making inquiries about her, decided to marry her to her son in America. Heranoush's parents told her they were interested in the marriage, but if she did not like the boy she need not marry him. In 1913, however, she did emigrate to America to marry; her mother-in-law lived with them. In 1915 her mother was killed, but her father and siblings escaped to America. Heranoush had four children, three girls and one boy. She was active in Protestant church and club activities.

11. Tsovinar Proodian Engoian

Born in 1894 in Erzeroum, the second daughter of three. Her father was a druggist; her mother was well educated. She attended

Hripsima Academy, graduating at fifteen. During the events of 1915 she lost all of her immediate family except two sisters. She came to America in 1922, married, and had five daughters and one son.

12. Arpeneh Boghikian Garboosian

Born in 1920 in Aleppo, Syria, and moved to Kessab in 1923, where her father taught school. She was the youngest of five children. She attended both elementary and secondary school. In 1936 she married, settled in Detroit, and had two sons. She worked as a beautician and was very active in the Armenian Relief Society.

13. Vartan Geragosian

Born about 1885 in Akor village, Kharpert province. His father died when he was young and his mother remarried. He did not attend school and made a living as a house painter. He married, but then left his wife to come to America. Having found a job at the Ford plant in Detroit, he brought her to America and they had three sons.

14. Flora Derbabian Gopigian

Born in 1893 in Gavra village, Sepastia region, one of three children. Her father died when she was very young, and her mother died when she was about ten. Her elder brother took over the household. She never attended school. She was betrothed at seven and married at sixteen. In 1910, after the birth of her first child, her husband emigrated to America to find work. During 1915 she was deported and walked from place to place for six years. A Turkish policeman kicked her little boy because he was crying and he died. She herself escaped death in the desert of Der-el-Zor with the help of two Turkish women, who dressed her as a Kurd with a veil. From there she reached British-held Aintab, where she found work as a servant. Through missionaries and the Armenian press in America, she located her husband. At his request she found his brother's children, and in 1921 she brought them to America. Reunited with her husband, she had two sons and a daughter.

15. Rebecca Kheteshian Hagopian

Born in 1901 in Zeitoun, one of seven children in a nuclear Protestant family. She attended elementary school in Zeitoun and continued her education at Central Girls' College at Marash on a scholarship. In 1922 her family had to leave for Syria, where she earned her college diploma at Aleppo in 1924. After teaching school in Kessab under difficult conditions for three years, she started to study nursing in Beirut. A few months later, in 1927, she married and came to America, first living in Pennsylvania and then in Detroit. She had two children and taught school.

16. Hripsima Nakushian Hoogasian

Born in 1891 in Kharpert, the elder of two girls. Her father died when she was very young, and her mother married a widower with four children. She remained with her grandmother, attending missionary schools in Kharpert. She married a skilled smith and had three children, but lost all of of them in 1915. Along with her mother, aunt, and sister, she reached Der-el-Zor and eventually India. With the help of the English Red Cross she reached America in 1921, remarried, and had three children, one of who became Susie Hoogasian Villa.

17. Euphapehyr Kachadoorian Hovsepian

Born in 1898 in Kharadigin, a village of one hundred households near Erzinjan, one of six children. Her father was a well-to-do farmer. She did not attend school. In 1915 Turkish friends from the same village helped the family by hiding them and employing the women as servants. In 1921, with the help of a brother-in-law, she came to Detroit, where she married a man from a village near her native village. They had one son.

18. Antaram Balian Janigian

Born in 1895 in Khorsana village, near Sepastia, one of eight children. Her fiancé left for America before 1915; she was deported to Syria. She came to North America in 1920, marrying in Montreal and then settling in Racine, Wisconsin. She and her husband were among the founders of the Saint Mesrop Armenian Church in Racine. They had two sons and a daughter.

19. Dikranouhi Eglinian (?) Jernukian

Born in July, 1908, in Sohngurlu, near Ankara, one of four children of a dry-goods merchant. Her mother was a Protestant, educated in a missionary school. In 1915 the Turks ordered that the affluent families should not be killed, but instead scattered among the villages; all the other Armenians were killed after they left town. Her family was spared, but their home and store were looted and demolished. When they returned to town, kind Turkish families gave them refuge. Her nephew reopened the store, but he was later deported and never seen again. After emigrating to America, she married; she had two daughters and one son.

20. Harioutioun Jernukian (husband of Informant 19)

Born on May 16, 1897, in Sabonji, a Turkish town ninety kilometers from Istanbul. He was the fourth child and first son of seven children born to his affluent Protestant parents. His father believed in the value of education, and all of his children received some formal schooling. Harioutioun was sent to a Turkish school in order to learn to read and write Turkish so that he could run the family business more effectively, and it was his knowledge of Turkish that saved his life during World War I. While he was serving as an officer in the Turkish army, he was instrumental in saving an Armenian village from a massacre. Fearing for his own life, he deserted to his hometown and then escaped to Greece with his mother, a brother, and a sister. In 1922, he and a sister emigrated to the United States.

21. Sahag Jevizian

Born on June 15, 1888, in Meghoozeek, a village of four hundred households near Erzunga, one of five children. His father wove Turkish towelling. Sahag attended elementary school and then went to work in the silkworm industry. At twenty he went to Rumania, after which, as a widower with a daughter, he moved on to the United States in 1910. He and his brother Barkev were the only surviving members of their family after 1915. In 1921 he married and had two sons and one daughter.

22. Arusiag Elibeyukian Kazanjian

Born in Sepastia in 1895, one of five children. Her father was a coffee merchant. She attended school until she was thirteen, and then spent two years earning a diploma in dressmaking. When the war began, her family sent her brother to America to escape conscription. She was the only other person in her immediate family to escape death in 1915. She had married by the beginning of the war, and by 1915 she had a baby a few months old. Her husband, who knew four languages, served as an interpreter for the Turks for four years. When the war was almost over they killed him. In 1915 she was deported; she reached Aintab when it was under British control and in 1920 joined her brother in New Haven, Connecticut. She remarried and had a daughter and a son.

23. Vartouhi Keteyian Korkian

Born in 1903 in Chengiler, a village of eighteen hundred households near Bursa, the eldest of three children. Her father was a stone mason and worked in a silkworm-breeding enterprise. In 1915 everyone in her immediate family died. She was entrusted to an old woman who sold her into slavery with an Arab family in Aleppo. She worked for them for four years and then escaped to an orphanage, later joining an aunt in Istanbul. Her husband, who had come from America to find a wife, married her and brought her to Detroit in 1920. They had five children.

24. Yeghisapert Zaroyhian Krikorian

Born in 1906 in Aralez, a village near Van of two hundred and fifty to three hundred households. She attended school only one winter. In 1915 her family found temporary safety in Russian Armenia, but they then returned to their native area. In 1918 they were again forced to flee, but, being unable to get into Russian Armenia, they went to Persia and then to Baghdad. In Baghdad she married a boy from her village, who brought her to Detroit in 1921. She had two daughters and one son.

25. Oskinaz Grjigian Maloian

Born in 1896 in Kughee, one of nine children. She did not attend school. In 1914 she married and had a child; both her husband and the child died in 1915. After five years of wandering, she reached her brother in Detroit in 1920. She remarried in 1923 and had one son and a daughter.

26. Mariam Makboorian Mossoian

Born in 1887 in Hakusdùn, a village of sixty households in the mountains near Kughee, the only daughter out of five children.

She was not sent to school, and married at seventeen. By 1915 she had four children, one of whom died in the midst of deportation. After living in the mountains and in Russian Armenia, she reached her family in Detroit in 1924.

27. Moorad Mooradian

Born in the early 1890s in Malatia, one of twelve children. He attended both Armenian and American schools and Yeprad College in Kharpert. At eighteen he came to America, where he worked for Ford Motor Company for thirty-five years and then helped establish a manufacturing concern. He was married and had four sons and a daughter. Moorad was noted for his sense of humor and keen mind.

28. Katoon Mouradian

Born in the 1890s in Palou, a village near Kharpert region. In 1915 her family fled to Aleppo, Syria. From there she emigrated, first to France, then to Canada, and finally to Detroit. She married and had two sons. She excelled as a storyteller, folk dancer, and folk healer.

29. Arsen Moushegian

Born about 1901 in Chanakjee village in Kughee. He attended Armenian schools until 1915. Kurds encamped in summer pastures at Bigol befriended him, and he stayed with them for two years. In about 1924, he reached Detroit with the help of a cousin. He did not marry. He operated a dry-cleaning shop and worked at the Ford plant.

30. Berjouhie Juldurian Nahnikian

Born in 1905 in Shabinkarahisar, near Sepastia, one of five children. She had two years of schooling. In 1915 she was separated from her family, and a Christian Kurdish family kept her for two years. She also spent a year with a Turkish family, and then joined her sister in Samsohn. Both came to America in 1921. She lived with her sister and brother-in-law until 1943, when she married.

31. Ardemis Tazian Hovagemian

Born in 1905 in Shabinkarahisar, near Sepastia, the youngest of three. She attended school for two years. Her brother found her and her sister working in a Turkish household. In 1920 she reached Detroit and married, but she had no children.

32. Armenouhie Tazian Derderian (older sister of Informant 31)

She taught kindergarten before 1915. In 1921 she came to the United States, married, and had three children.

33. Levon Nahnikian (husband of Informant 30)

Born in 1892 in Shabinkarahisar, near Sepastia, one of four children, the son of a dry-goods merchant. He attended school and learned the trade of shoemaking. In 1912 he was drafted, but after six months he deserted and came to America. After working in various shoe factories, he opened a dry-cleaning and shoe-repair shop in Detroit. In 1943 he married, but he had no children.

34. Gevork Najarian

Born in 1895 in Severeg, the son of a cabinet maker. He attended school until he was seventeen. In 1915 a Turkish army major who was a friend of his father saved his life. He married in 1917 and escaped with his wife to Aleppo, Syria, in 1922. They had four children. In 1930 they moved to France, and in 1957 to America.

35. Toumia Najarian (wife of Informant 34)

Born in Severeg, the third of five children. Her father was a well-to-do gunsmith. She attended school until the age of fourteen. In 1915 her family gave money to a Turkish family to hide her. In 1917 she married.

36. Noami Gulesarian Nazarian

Born in 1897 in Kurdbelem, Gayve district, near Istanbul, one of six children. She attended elementary school and then worked in the local silk factory until she was eighteen. In 1915 she went to Konya; she then worked as a dressmaker in Istanbul. In 1926 she married and had one daughter.

37. Satenik Babaian Ossian

Born in 1900 in Akhalkalakh in Georgia, a town of three hundred households. She was one of six children; her father was a baker. She attended Armenian parochial school for five years, and then sewing school. In 1920 she married; she had her first child in February, 1921, on the S.S. *Alexander* as it sailed to America. She named the child Alex. Three more children followed.

38. Mamigon Ossian (husband of Informant 37)

Born in 1895 in Chanakjee village, in Kughee, in a gerdastan with twenty-five members. He emigrated to Saint Louis, Missouri, in 1913. In 1917 he returned to his homeland, and after World War I he worked for Near East Relief in Akhalkalakh, Georgia, distributing food to needy Armenians. There he met and married Satenik Babaian in 1920. In 1921 they returned to the United States. Mamigon worked for the Plymouth Division of Chrysler Corporation for twenty-nine years.

39. Naomi Arslanian Ouzounian

Born around 1901 in Hajin, the daughter of a Protestant landowner who had Turkish peasants working in his fields and vineyards. After 1915 she went to Istanbul, where she graduated from a teachers' college. In 1926 she came to America and married a man from her hometown who owned a tailoring and cleaning shop in Chicago. She taught French in the Chicago schools. She had two daughters.

40. Pepperone Pashian

Born in Tortan village, near Kemakh. She married a boy from her village and had a son, who was killed in 1915. In America she had two daughters.

41. Harootiun Phinjanian

Born in 1892 in Karakehoy, a village of about sixty households, near Adana. His father died early. He attended elementary school. At about nineteen he married. In 1913 he went to America, leaving his pregnant wife, but two years later both his wife and their daughter died. He remained in America and remarried in 1929; he had a son and a daughter. He worked in the Ford factory.

42. Haiganoush Khezarjian Saatjian

Born in 1898 in Tezeli, a village of fifteen hundred households near Yozgat, one of four surviving children. Her father owned a general store. She attended American missionary schools until 1915 and became a Protestant. For the next five years she sewed shirts for the Turkish army and worked as a nurse in the American hospital at Adana, where she met her future husband. She married in 1920 and came to Detroit as a new bride, accompanied by her mother-in-law (who lived with the couple until her death at ninety-nine). Her husband worked in a factory and as a self-employed tailor, and later went into the hotel business. They had two daughters.

43. Kapriel Saboonjian

Born in 1895 in Van, one of five children in an affluent family. His father was killed the same year. In 1915 he retreated with Russian troops to Erevan. In 1921 he went to join his sister in Istanbul, and two years later he settled near her in Detroit. There he worked as a shoe-repairer, married, and had two daughters and one son.

44. Nevart Siroonian Sarkisian

Born in 1901 in Kughee, one of two children. While her father worked in Istanbul, she and her mother stayed with his gerdastan. This gerdastan was involved in the Armenian underground, and guns and ammunition were stored in the house. Her uncle was arrested, tortured for four months and executed. In 1915, most of the men of Kughee were killed and the women and children deported. She worked for two years in a hospital and then at an American orphanage in Kharpert. In 1925, she married and settled in Detroit. Soon afterward her mother and brother crossed the Atlantic. She had two sons.

45. Norayan Sarookanian

Born in 1908 in the village of Vardo-Gundemir, the youngest of six children. She had been in school only one year when her family was killed. A Kurdish family saved her life; she worked for them and then moved with them to Kharpert. She took refuge with American missionaries. After living in orphanages in Syria and Greece, she reached Canada in 1924. In Detroit she married and had two children.

46. Mida Ipekjian Semerjian

Born in 1900 in Amasia, the only girl and the youngest of six children. Two of her brothers had emigrated to the United States before 1915. Her father, an affluent silk manufacturer and a Protestant, had many friends in the German colony who helped her when her immediate family was annihilated. After emigrating to the United States, she attended school, married, and had two daughters. She became a talented cook and organizer for Armenian causes.

47. Mariam Juskalian Serabian

Born in the 1870s, and widowed in her late twenties, she and her two daughters were made destitute during the massacres in 1895. She married a man from Hussenig and bore a son. After much suffering during World War I, Mariam and her son emigrated to America in 1923. She was a fortune-teller, a folk healer, and Susie Hoogasian Villa's grandmother.

48. Varder Zakarian

Born in the late 1890s in Harseg village, near Kharpert. She married and had two daughters. Her husband emigrated to America, where he died. She and one daughter survived with the help of missionaries. They reached Detroit, where she remarried and had two sons.

GLOSSARY

achkee looysee, light unto the eyes, congratulations
akhor, stable
al (pl. *alk*), malevolent spirit(s)
amot, shameful
aror, scratch plow, lightweight plow
asa bash, master of ceremonies (*bash* is Turkish)
azkasehr, "to love one's nationality," patriotic

badeev, honor
bastegh, dried fruit roll made from thickened fruit juice
bulgher, cracked wheat

cheengeneh, cheap, stingy (Turkish word meaning gypsy)

dahn deegeen, wife of family head
dahneek, roof
dahn hatz, bread for the household, *lavash,* very thin bread
dahnooder, man of the household, owner of the house
dahn pesah, son-in-law living in the home of his in-laws
daross, good fortune
davoul and *zourna,* drum and fifelike instruments
doon-mnah, "left at home," old maid
doshag, woolen mattress

dzour bsag, irregular wedding, e.g., wedding occurring during Lent or other unacceptable time

ehnad[utiun], stubbornness (Turkish with Armenian ending)

Frankee aghd, "French dirt," syphilis

Gaghant Baba, "Father Christmas," Santa Claus

gaghantel-ing, "Christmas gifting," visiting to extend Christmas greetings

gahl, area of hard-packed earth used for threshing

gangar, vegetable similar to artichoke

gerdastan, family clan, immediate family which can be traced to same parents/grandparents

ges bsag, "half wedding ceremony"

goashgoor, dried dung

gom, shed for sheep and goats

gunkahyr, godfather at a baptism or wedding. See also *kavor.*

gutan, heavy plow

guyr, blind

hadig, large, boiled, whole wheat grain

hamkal, plowing unit

hamest, unassuming, modest

hamozel, "to persuade" with advice, to sweet talk

Hampartzoum, Ascension Day

harakash, plowing unit

hars, bride, daughter-in-law

harsaneek, wedding reception

hereseh, dish of shredded lamb and barley, combined by lengthy stirring process while being slowly cooked

hokeh hatz, "bread for the soul"

jagadakeer, "what is written on the forehead," one's destiny, fate

jarbeeg, clever, shrewd

katah, firm rolls made of flour, eggs, and butter, richer than bread

kavor, godfather at wedding, baptism

kavorgeen, wife of godfather

kerpeech, large mud bricks (Turkish)

khachi gunkahyr, godfather of the cross

khach kavor, godfather of the cross

khach kuyr, god-sister

khach yeghpayr, god-brother

khavoorma, browned, cooked meat prepared for storage and covered and sealed in its own fat

khnamee, in-law, includes everyone in family or gerdastan, can include entire village of bride

khnamoutiun, in-law relationship

khosk arenk, "we have received their work," verbal commitment or promise

khumash, fine cloth (Turkish)

khuradel, to give a moral lesson

lavash, thin bread baked in a *toneer.* See also *dahn hatz.*

madagh, offering, sacrifice

madzoon, yogurt

manana, "manna," sweet lichen, probably *Lecanora esculenta*

marak, storage area for hay

maran, storeroom for dry foodstuffs

marantz yertal, visit to mother's household

meechnordt, "go between," matchmaker

mehron, holy oil

Merelotz, memorial day for the dead, Monday after Easter

moonch, silent, speechless, "silent period" of daughter-in-law in home of in-laws

nakhantz, jealous, envious

nahabed, head of a village, patriarch

nor harsnutiun, newlywed, period of initiation for a new daughter-in-law

nshan, "sign," ring or other ornament given to the future bride at betrothal

nshkhark, holy wafer

oda, living room, parlor (Turkish)

ojakh, hearth, wall fireplace, by extension, a household (Turkish)

ogormatz hokeen, "dear departed soul"

pag, open courtyard

paklava, pastry with many fine layers of dough, honey, and nuts (Turkish)

paree, good, just

Pareengentahn, religious event occurring at beginning of Lent, similar to Mardi Gras

petak (pl. *petakner*), large, unfired pottery containers for storing dry foodstuffs, beehive

pilaf, rice or wheat dish with various seasonings

pokhint, a delicacy made of flour and butter, sweetened with honey

rakhee, alcoholic drink derived from raisins (Turkish); *oghee* (Armenian)

sadj hatz, flat bread, about eighteen inches in diameter, baked on metal pan (*sadj* is Turkish)

sanahyr, father of child who received services of godfather

sedeer, platform covered with pillows set against a wall, daybed (Turkish)

tagh, "quarter," section of a village or city

tahn, drink made of madzoon diluted with water

toneer (pl. *toneerner*), sunken fireplace dug out of the ground

undanik, nuclear family

Vartavar, joyous, ritual observance occurring ninety-eight days
   after Easter
veejag, fortune, condition, custom of drawing a fortune from a
   container

yazma, kind of veil (Turkish)
yertik, smokehole, vent, dormer
yukluk, storage area for bedding

zooroutznel, to tease, encourage talking by a young child

NOTES

Preface

1. Among good recent histories of Armenia are Louise Z. Nalbandian, *The Armenian Revolutionary Movement: The Development of Armenian Political Parties through the Nineteenth Century* (Berkeley, Calif., 1963); Sirarpie Der Nessessian, *The Armenians* (London, 1969); and David M. Lang, *Armenia: Cradle of Civilization* (London, 1970).

2. The modern Armenian church, sometimes called the Gregorian church, is still a distinctively national church; its rites are basically those of the other Eastern Orthodox churches, although with some differences. It is organized under its own patriarch. See, for example, Patriarch Malachia Ormanian, *The Church of Armenia*, new ed. (London, 1955); H. Pasdermasjian, *Histoire de l'Arménie*, 2d ed. (Paris, 1964); and Aziz S. Atiya, *A History of Eastern Christianity* (London, 1967).

3. Informants 15 and 42.

4. Lang, *Armenia*, p. 286.

5. Ibid., p. 287

6. Hamaskaine Armenian Cultural Association, *An Anthology of Historical Writings on the Armenian Massacres of 1915* (Beirut, 1971) contains excerpts from the writings of Viscount James Bryce, Arnold J. Toynbee, Herbert Adams Gibbons, Henry Morgenthau, and Fridjhof Nansen, and an extensive bibliography.

7. See, for example, Kerop Bedoukian, *Some of Us Survived: The Story of an Armenian Boy* (New York, 1978).

Chapter 1

1. In Max Weber's classification, such forms of government are called *patrimonial* (*The Theory of Social and Economic Organization* [Glencoe, Ill., 1947], pp. 346–47). Richard Pipes develops this theme in *Russia under the Old Regime* (New York, 1974), esp. pp. 1–47. Fernand Braudel collected evidence of the weakness of such governments, particularly in mountainous areas, in *The Mediterranean and the Mediterranean World in the Age of Philip II*, 2d ed. (New York, 1976), 1:38–40, 2:692–93; there is also mention of it in Kemal H. Karpat, ed., *The Ottoman State and Its Place in World History* (Leiden, 1974), pp. 10, 72.

2. M. V. Akopian, "Obshchinnye skhod v sisteme sotsial'noi organizatsii armianskoi sel'skoi obshchiny poreformennogo perioda," *Lraber obshchestvennykh nauk* 2 (1975):37–46.

3. E. T. Karapetian, *Rodstvennaia Gruppa 'Azg' u Armian* (Erevan, 1966), pp. 49–58.

4. Ibid., pp. 63–140.

5. Jacques Heers, *Familial Clans in the Middle Ages* (New York, 1977); John Davis, *People of the Mediterranean* (London, 1977), pp. 167–238; Paul Stirling, *Turkish Village* (New York, 1965), pp. 26, 155–62; Edit Fel and Tamas Hofer, *Proper Peasants: Traditional Life in a Hungarian Village* (Chicago, 1969), p. 152; Joel Halpern, *A Serbian Village* (New York, 1958), pp. 150–57; John K. Campbell, *Honour, Family, and Patronage* (Oxford, 1964), pp. 50–57; Paul J. Magnarella, *The Peasant Venture* (Boston, 1979), pp. 29–30.

6. S. D. Lisitsian, "Ocherki etnografii dorevoliutsionni: Armenii," *Kavkazskii Etnograficheskii Sbornik* [Moscow] 1 (1955):257–58; Karapetian, *Rodstevennaia Gruppa 'Azg'*, pp. 66–67.

7. E. T. Karapetian, *Armianskia Semeinaia Obshchina* (Erevan, 1958), pp. 38–41; "Armiane," *Narody Kavkaza* 2 (1962):524.

8. M. O. Kosven, *Semeinaia Obshchina i Patronimia* (Moscow, 1963); Robert F. Byrne, ed., *Communal Families in the Balkans: The Zadruga* (Notre Dame, Ind., 1976); R. L. Kharadze, *Gruzinskaia Semeinaia Obshchina*, 2 vols. (Tbilisi, 1960, 1961).

9. Karapetian, *Armianskaya Semeinaia Obshchina*, "Ocherki etnografii," pp. 91–103; Lisitsian, pp. 232–45; V. H. Bdoyan, *Hay Azgagrutyun: Hamarot Urvagits* (Erevan, 1974), pp. 124–31, 158–64; "Armiane," *Narody Kavkaza*, 2 vol. pp. 524–26.

10. Lisitsian, "Ocherki etnografii," pp. 202–3.

11. James Mellaart, *Çatal Hüyük* (New York, 1967), pp. 67–69.

12. August von Haxthausen, *Transcaucasia* (London, 1854), p. 212.

13. J. O. Barrows, *On Horseback in Cappodocia* (Boston, 1884), p. 130.

14. Bdoyan, *Hay Azgagrutyun*, p. 73.

15. The yertik is mentioned in the Armenian folk epic *David of Sassoon* (trans. A. K. Shalian, Athens, Ohio, 1964, p. 308). By implication, the Armenians were building similar houses in the ninth century, when the epic took final form. The yertik was also found in dwellings at Çatal Hüyük in the seventh to sixth millennia B.C. (Mellaart, *Çatal Hüyük*, p. 56).

16. Lisitsian, "Ocherki etnografii," pp. 204–9.

17. Robert N. C. G. Curzon Zouche, *Armenia: A Year at Erzeroom* (London, 1854), p. 44.

18. Lisitsian, "Ocherki etnografii," pp. 210–13.

19. Mardiros Ananikian, "Armenian Mythology," in *Mythology of All Races*, ed. John MacCulloch (Boston, 1925), p. 55; Manuk Abegian, *Der Armenische Volksglaube* (Leipzig, 1899), p. 69.

20. Clarence E. Ussher, *An American Physician in Turkey* (Boston, 1917), pp. 12–13.

Chapter 2

1. Lisitsian, "Ocherki etnografii," p. 199.

2. James Barton, *Daybreak in Turkey* (Boston, 1980), p. 233; Haxthausen, *Transcaucasia*, p. 181; Barrows, *On Horseback in Cappodocia*, pp. 206–8.

3. Bdoyan, *Hay Azgagrutyun*, p. 46.

4. V. H. Bdoyan, *Erkragordzakan Mshakuyte Hayastanum* (Erevan, 1972), pp. 257–65.

5. Catherine D. Smith, *Western Mediterranean Europe* (London, 1979) p. 197.

6. Bdoyan, *Hay Azgagrutyun*, pp. 63–64; Lisitsian, "Ocherki etnografii," p. 201.

7. "Armiane," *Narody Kavkaza*, vol. 2, p. 471.

8. Professor Parrot identified this lichen on his trip to Mount Ararat and noted that the natives of the area ate it (U. P. Hedrick, ed., *Sturtevant's Edible Plants of the World* [New York, 1972], p.330).

9. Parsadan Ter Mowsesjanz, "Der Armenische Bauernhaus," *Anthropologische Gesellschaft in Wien* 22 (1892):125–72; Barrows, *On Horseback in Cappodocia*, pp. 120–22; Mrs. W. M. Ramsey, *Every-Day Life in Turkey* ((London, 1897), pp. 56–57. The quotation is from Ramsey.

10. See Hoogasian-Villa, *One Hundred Armenian Tales*, pp. 354–55 for the process of inflating, treating, and forming a sheepskin into a waterproof container. E. J. Davis, describing a goatskin churn in *Life in Asiatic Turkey* (London, 1879), adds, "full of milk, it is suspended to a triangle of three poles. The women . . . work it up and down" (p. 121).

11. This practice is confirmed by Mrs. E. C. A. Schneider, *Letters from Broosa, Asia Minor* (Chambersburg, Pa., 1846), p. 84, and Cyrus Hamlin, *Among the Turks* (New York, 1878), p. 174. Even today, older Armenians in Detroit sit on a stool in the bathtub, dip water with a pail, and pour it over themselves.

12. The information in this and the following three paragraphs is based on Lisitsian, "Ocherki etnografii," pp. 222–32.

13. Barrows, *On Horseback in Cappadocia*, p. 116.

14. Helene Balfet, "Bread in Some Regions of the Mediterranean: A Contribution to the Study of Eating Habits," in *Gastronomy*, ed. Margaret L. Arnott (The Hague, 1975), pp. 305–14.

15. The closest parallels to Armenian material culture outside of Anatolia were found in Iran, a region where timber also is scarce. See Clara C. Rice, *Persian Women and Their Ways* (London, 1923), esp. pp. 56–58, 168–76.

16. Jean-Louis Flandrin, *Families in Former Times* (Cambridge, 1979), pp.98–101.

17. Paul Stirling, *Turkish Village* (New York, 1965), p. 22; Edit Fel and Tamas Hofer, *Proper Peasants: Traditional Life in a Hungarian Village* (Chicago, 1969).

18. See for example, Mary Matossian, "In the Beginning, God Was a Woman," *Journal of Social History* (Spring 1973):325–43; and Lucienne Roubin, "Male Space and Female Space within the Provençal Community," *Rural Society in France*, R. Forster and O. Ranum (Baltimore, 1977), pp. 152–80.

Chapter 3

1. Ter Mowsesjanz, "Armenische Bauernhaus," p. 139.

2. Haxthausen, *Transcaucasia*, p. 225, verifies that marriage was forbidden within seven degrees of blood relation.

3. Bdoyan, *Hay Azgagrutyun*, p. 137.

4. Confirmed ibid., pp. 139–40.

5. Henry Van Lennep, *Bible Lands: Their Modern Customs and Manners* (New York, 1875), pp. 545–47, confirms that the essentials of a wedding in the region were: toilet of bride done in the presence of friends; henna applied to hands and feet of bride; bride taken to bath; plaintive song on parting from maternal home; davoul and zourna used throughout the proceedings. The expense of the bridal attire, according to Van Lennep, was borne by the bridegroom.

6. Armenians have many stories in which an apple is a cure for barrenness; it is also used by the hero or heroine as a means of indicating whom they have selected as a mate. See Hoogasian-Villa, *One Hundred Armenian Tales*, pp. 71–72.

7. Barrows, *On Horseback in Cappodocia*, p. 283, says that if more than one room were available, men and women were seated separately.

8. Henry Van Lennep, *Travels in Little Known Parts of Asia Minor*, 2 vols. (London, 1870), 1:274, verifies this. On 1:270, he says that a ten-year-old boy imitates the bridegroom and is known as a mock groom, but the Detroit informants did not verify this custom.

9. Lisitsian, "Ocherki etnografii," pp. 235–41.

10. Edmund Schneeweis, *Serbokroatische Volkskunde* (Berlin, 1961), p. 81.

11. Alexander Grigolia, *Custom and Justice in the Caucasus: The Georgian Highlanders* (Philadelphia, 1939), pp. 69–70.

12. John Gulick, *The Middle East: An Anthropological Perspective* (Pacific Palisades, Calif., 1976), p. 184; Johannes Piprek, *Slawische Brautwerbungs- und Hochzeitsgebrauche* (Stuttgart, 1914), p. 174; Bernard Stern, *The Scented Garden* (New York, 1934), pp. 158–61; Henri Massé, *Persian Beliefs and Customs* (New Haven, Conn., 1954), p. 61; D. K. Zelenin, *Russische (Ostslawissche) Volkskunde* (Leipzig, 1927), pp. 209–10; Jane Schneider and Peter Schneider, *Culture and Political Economy in Western Sicily* (New York, 1976), p. 91; Stirling, *Turkish Village*, p. 185; Magnarella, *Peasant Venture*, pp. 49–50.

13. Sidney W. Mintz and Eric R. Wolf, "An Analysis of Ritual Co-parenthood (compadrazgo)," *Southwestern Journal of Anthropology* 6 (1950):341–68; Eugene A. Hammel, *Alternative Social Structures and Ritual Relations in the Balkans* (Englewood Cliffs, N.J., 1968); Mary E. Durham, *Some Tribal Origins, Laws, and Customs of the Balkans* (London, 1928), pp. 304–5; Julian Pitt-Rivers, "Ritual Kinship in the Mediterranean: Spain and the Balkans," in *Mediterranean Family Structures*, J. G. Peristiany (Cambridge, 1976), pp. 317–34; C. G. Chapman, *Milocca: A Sicilian Village* (London, 1973), pp. 115–22; Fel and Hofer, *Proper Peasants*, p. 163; Campbell, *Honour, Family, and Patronage*, pp. 218–21; Halpern, *Serbian Village*, p. 161; Davis, *People of the Mediterranean*, pp. 223–38.

14. A. K. Sertel, "Ritual Kinship in Eastern Turkey," *Anthropological Quarterly* 44, no. 1 (1971):35–50; Paul J. Magnarella and Orhan Turkdogan, "Descent, Affinity, and Ritual Relations in Eastern Turkey," *American Anthropologist* 75, no. 5 (1973):1626–33.

15. Stirling, *Turkish Village*, pp. 112, 189, 210–12.

Chapter 4

1. Armenians feared that evil spirits endangered newlyweds during the first forty days after marriage; therefore the bride did not go to the spring for water and remained indoors after dark (Minas Tcheraz, *L'Orient inédit* [Paris, 1912], p. 153; Lucy Garnett, *The Women of Turkey and Their Folklore: Christian Women* [London, 1894], pp. 230–46, 316, 326). Manuk Abeghian, *Der Armenische Volksglaube* (Leipzig, 1899), p. 91, describes the belief that since newlyweds were especially sensitive to evil spirits and evil forces, they should carry a closed lock or closed knife on their persons at all time, because metal protects against these dangers. He also says that when the couple entered their house together for the first time, the sign of the cross should be made at the entrance with a sword, which would make it impossible for evil spirits to enter the household.

2. Haxthausen, *Transcaucasia*, p. 228; Schneider, *Letters from Broosa*, p. 78; James Creagh, *Armenians, Koords, and Turks*, 2 vols. (London, 1890), 2:118, confirm this.

3. Van Lennep, *Travels*, 1:276, says that this period of silence sometimes lasted fifteen to twenty years; Ussher, *American Physician*, p. 13, cites the case of a woman who had been married for forty years and still was not permitted to speak to her father-in-law. However, Informant 8, from Ghermehr, near Caesarea, said that her father made a new daughter-in-law talk to him on her wedding day. He asked her a question and commanded her to answer; she kissed his hand and spoke to him from that time on.

4. Haxthausen, *Transcaucasia*, p. 228; Creagh, *Armenians, Koords, and Turks*, 2:116, verifies this.

5. Hoogasian-Villa, *One Hundred Armenian Tales*, discussion and references, pp. 60–62, 72.

6. G. Aharonian, *Husseynik* (Boston, 1966), pp. 73–74, says that the old beliefs show that although the souls of the dead rose to heaven, their bodies remained behind and lived a material life. They were aware of the respect given their graves; thus the living could influence the tranquility of the dead, who in turn could influence the fortunes of the family.

7. See also Hoogasian-Villa, *One Hundred Armenian Tales*, p. 235, for a folktale in which chick peas are used to cure barrenness.

8. Bdoyan, *Hay Azgagrutyun*, p. 128. According to Paul Essabel, "The Door and Threshold in Armenian Folklore," *Western Folklore Journal* 20 (1961):271, the wife was held responsible for both infertility and failure to produce male children.

9. Mrs. John Elyah Blunt, *The People of Turkey*, 2 vols. (London, 1878), 2:21.

10. See Hoogasian-Villa, *One Hundred Armenian Tales*, pp. 64–66, for a discussion of alk; see also pp. 352–54 for a folktale about these spirits.

11. Shalian, trans., *David of Sassoun*, p. 15.

12. According to Informant 27, from Pula, holy water was made in a huge golden kettle. All kinds of flowers were placed in this kettle, which was then set aside somewhere clean. Priests prayed for forty days and forty nights while the flowers boiled in the kettle; at the end of that time, the holy water was ready to be strained.

13. Tavernier, *Collections of Travels through Turkey into Persia and the East Indies* (London, 1684), p. 171, affords a similar picture from two centuries earlier.

14. Halpern, *Serbian Village*, p. 199; Joe E. Pierce, *Life in a Turkish Village* (New York, 1964), p. 83.

15. Magnarella, *Peasant Venture*, p. 52; Campbell, *Honour, Family, and Patronage*, p. 154; D. K. Zelenin, *Russische (Ostslawisch) Volkskunde* (Leipzig, 1927), p. 293; Henri Massé, *Persian Beliefs and Customs* (New Haven, Conn., 1954), pp. 14, 23; Julian Morgenstern, *Rites of Birth, Marriage, Death, and Kindred Occasions among the Semites* (New York, 1973), pp. 27–28.

16. Alexander Grigolia, *Custom and Justice in the Caucasus: The Georgian Highlanders* (Philadelphia, 1939), pp. 99–106.

17. Massé, *Persian Beliefs*, pp. 21, 39; Morgenstern, *Rites*, p. 20.

18. Hilma Granqvist, *Birth and Childhood among the Arabs* (Helsinki, 1947), p. 114.

19. Ibid., pp. 97–98, 242; Morgenstern, *Rites*, pp. 7–9, 13–15, Mary M. McLaughlin, "Survivors and Surrogates: Children and Parents from the Ninth to the Thirteenth Centuries," in *The History of Childhood*, edited by Lloyd de Mause (New York, 1974), p. 133; M. J. Tucker, "The Child as Beginning and End: Fifteenth and Sixteenth Century English Childhood," ibid., p. 239.

Chapter 5

1. Martha B. Atikian and Hagop Atikian, *Armenian Names* (n.p., 1973) has been extremely valuable for the information about names and naming practices included in my text.

2. Confirmed by Frederik Davis Greene, *The Rule of the Turk* (New York, 1896), p. 160.

3. According to Informant 3, from Karaghil, near Moush, hadig was made and sent to school with the children on the anniversary of the grandfather's death.

4. V. Ia. Propp, *Russkie agrarnye prazdniki* (Leningrad, 1963), pp. 15–16.

5. Van Lennep, *Travels*, 1:256, says that it was improper for a mother to show affection for her child; she could only kiss it in private. The grandmother controlled the child. Van Lennep affords much information about intrafamilial relationships.

6. Barrows, *On Horseback in Cappodocia,* pp. 83–84, remarks: "Armenians feel that others' ignorance and circumstances are always to be taken advantage of. If one does not do this, others believe that he does not have the capacity to take care of the opportunities presented to him. They say, 'If a man's eyes are not open [so that he can see what is going on] that is his business [whatever happens to him can be justified]'."

7. Informants 15, 23, 30, 31, 39, 41, and 44 described the schoolteacher's disciplinary role, saying that the family taught values and the school reinforced them. Severe physical punishment could occur at school, and Informant 15 reported that parents taking their child to school for the first time would say, "The flesh is yours; don't abuse the bones." According to Informant 41, from Karakehoy, if a child continually misbehaved at home, his parents might tell the schoolteacher, who would then punish him. Apparently physical isolation of the child was used as a punishment as well as spanking.

8. Some of the important values which appear in stories included in Hoogasian-Villa, *One Hundred Armenian Tales,* are: the belief in fate (pp. 322–48); the desirability of cleverness (pp. 376–79); the importance of truth (pp. 345–48); the love of children (pp. 350–51); the necessity of hard work (pp. 327–28); the necessity of honor (pp. 331–38); the necessity of patience (pp. 175–80); postponement of immediate pleasure (pp. 340–44); respect for age (pp. 255–66).

9. Ernestine Friedl, *Vasilika, a Village in Modern Greece* (New York, 1963), pp. 78–80; John C. Lawson, *Modern Greek Folklore and Ancient Greek Religion* (New Hyde Park, N.Y., 1964), p. 31; Richard Blum and Eva Blum, *The Dangerous Hour* (New York, 1970), pp. 221–22. Jane Schneider and Peter Schneider, *Culture and Political Economy in Western Sicily* (New York, 1976), pp. 82–86; Sania Hamady, *Temperament and Character of the Arabs* (New York, 1960), pp. 36–37, 100–101; Norman Jacobs, *The Sociology of Development: Iran as an Asian Case Study* (New York, 1966), p. 252–63.

10. Davis, *People of the Mediterranean,* pp. 100–101; Jane Schneider, "Of Vigilance and Virgins," *Ethnology* 9, no. 1 (1971):1–24.

Chapter 6

1. Keith Thomas, *Religion and the Decline of Magic* (New York, 1971); Peter Burke, *Popular Culture in Early Modern Europe* (New York, 1978).

2. Bdoyan, *Hay Azgagrutyun,* pp. 206–7; Nvard Yernchakyan, "Lusine Hay zhoghovrda-kan havataliknerum ev sovorwitnerum," *Lraber Hasarakakan Gitutyunneri,* no. 2 (1979), pp. 53–60.

3. V. H. Bdoyan, *Yerkragortsakan Mshakuyte Hayastanum* (Erevan, 1972), esp. pp. 436–37; Bdoyan, *Hay Azgagrutyun,* pp. 46, 198.

4. Lisitsian, "Ocherki etnografii," p. 257; Bdoyan, *Hay Azgagrutyun,* p. 201; K. V. Melik-Pashayan, *Anahit Ditsuhu Pashtamunke* (Erevan, 1963).

5. Melik-Pashayan, *Anahit,* pp. 59, 154–55, 143; Lucy Garnett, *The Women of Turkey and Their Folklore: Christian Women* (London, 1894), p. 230. According to Bdoyan, *Hay Azgagrutyun,* "Anahit" was a name of non-Armenian origin given to an indigenous Armenian female deity. He suggests that her original name was Nari (p. 218). The center of her cult was at Eriza (Erez) in the Yekeghats (Akilisene) region (Melik-Pashayan, *Anahit,* p. 88). In the Zoroastrian religion, Anahit was the goddess of springs and rivers and was invoked by nubile girls, women in labor, and nursing mothers (James Hastings, ed., *Encyclopedia of Religion and Ethics,* vol. 1 (Edinburgh, 1908), p. 414). In recent times the Uzbeks asso-

ciated Anahit with sacred springs and with the Ardvi (Oxus, Amu-Darya) River (G. P. Snesarov, "Remnants of Pre-Islamic Beliefs and Rituals Aming the Khorezm Uzbeks," *Soviet Anthropology and Archaeology* 13, no. 1 [Summer 1974]:27; and 13, no. 2 [Fall 1974]:3–32).

6. Abeghian, *Armenische Volksglaube,* pp. 61–62; see also Hoogasian-Villa, *One Hundred Armenian Tales,* pp. 253–55, 430–33, for stories about the magical qualities of water.

7. Bdoyan, *Hay Azgagrutyun,* pp. 213, 201.

8. Ibid., p. 213.

9. Ibid., pp. 201–2; Lisitsian, "Ocherki etnografii,;" pp. 257–58.

10. Barrows, *On Horseback in Cappodocia,* p. 203 also speaks of holy shrubs on which pieces of rag were tied. People hoped thereby to be cured of diseases, especially fevers and agues. See also Lisitsian, "Ocherki etnografii," p. 257.

11. Bdoyan, *Hay Azgagrutyun,* pp. 208–210.

12. See Hoogasian-Villa, *One Hundred Armenian Tales,* p. 67, for a discussion of saint snakes.

13. Bdoyan, *Hay Azgagrutyun,* pp. 209–10.

14. D. K. Zelenin, "Magicheskaia funktsiia primitivnykh orudii," *Investiia Akademii Nauk, Otdelenie Obshchestvennykh Nauk,* no. 6 (1931), p. 397; S. A. Tokarev, *Religioznye Verovanie Vostochnoslavianskikh Narodov* (Moscow, 1957), pp. 74–77; A. N. Afanas'ev, *Poeticheskie vozreniia slavian na prirodu,* 3 vols. (Moscow, 1865–69), 1:139–45; Oskar Loorits, *Grundzuge des estnische Volksglaubens* (Lund, 1951), pp. 71–73; G. P. Snesarov, "Remnants of Pre-Islamic Beliefs and Rituals among the Khorezm Uzbeks," *Soviet Anthropology and Archaeology* 12, no. 4 (Spring, 1974):14–16; Mircea Eliade, *Patterns in Comparative Religion* (New York, 1964), pp. 220–22; Afanas'ev, *Poeticheskie vozreniia slavian na prirodu,* 2: 170–71; John C. Lawson, *Modern Greek Folklore and Ancient Greek Religion* (New Hyde Park, N.Y. 1964), pp. 159–62; Jonas Balys, "Die Sagen von den litauischen Feen," *Die Nachbarn,* vol. 1 (Gottingen, 1948), pp. 31–71; V. K. Sokolva, *Vesenne-Letnie Kalendarnye Obriady: Russkikh, Ukraintsev, i Belorusov* (Moscow, 1979), pp. 213–23; B. A. Rybakov, "The Rusalki and the God Simargl-Pereplut," *Soviet Anthropology and Archaeology* 6, no. 4 (Spring 1968):34–59; G. P. Snesarov, "Remnants of Pre-Islamic Beliefs and Rituals among the Khorem Uzbeks," *Soviet Anthropology and Archaeology* 10, no. 1 (Summer 1971):18–20.

15. Matossian, "In the Beginning, God Was a Woman," pp. 324–43; Afanas'ev, *Poeticheskie vozreniia slavian na prirodu,* 1:231–32; Richard and Eva Blum, *The Dangerous Hour* (New York, 1970), p. 324; John Abbot, *The Keys to Power* (London, 1932), pp. 190, 243–44, 324; V. Iu. Leshchenko, "The Position of Women in the Light of Religious-Domestic Taboos among the East Slavic Peoples in the Nineteenth and Early Twentieth Centuries," *Soviet Anthropology and Archaeology* 17, no. 3 (Winter 1978–79):22–40; Grigolia, *Custom and Justice,* p. 37; Massé, *Persian Beliefs,* p. 262.

16. William V. Crooke, *The Popular Religion and Folklore of Northern India,* vol. 1 (Westminster, 1896), p. 69.

17. Zelenin, "Magicheskaia funktsiia primitivnykh orduii," pp. 326, 329.

18. Tokarev, *Religionznye Verovanie Vostochnoslavianakikh Narodov,* pp. 68–70; Zelenin, "Magicheskaia funktsiia primitivnykh orduii," p. 327; Snesarov, "Remnants of Pre-Islamic Belief" (Spring 1974), pp. 10–11; Grigolia, *Custom and Justice,* p. 57; Maria Leach, ed., *Funk and Wagnalls Standard Dictionary of Folklore, Mythology, and Legend* (1949–50), p. 633; Martin P. Nilsson, *Greek Folk Religion* (New York, 1961), pp. 72–73.

19. "Armiane," *Narody Kavkaza,* vol. 2, pp. 141, 318, 411; Francis W. Carter, ed., *An Historical Geography of the Balkans* (London, 1977), p. 94.

20. Abbott, *Keys to Power*, pp. 325–28; Massé, *Persian Beliefs*, pp. 220–23, 502; Crooke, *Popular Religion and Folklore*, pp. 161–62; Arthur J. Evans, *The Mycenaean Tree and Pillar Cult* (London, 1901), p. 103; James M. Mackinlay, *Folklore of Scottish Lochs and Springs* (Glasgow, 1893), pp. 233–34; John Rhys, *Celtic Folklore, Welsh and Manx* (Oxford, 1901), pp. 322, 354–62; Robert C. Hope, *The Legendary Lore of Holy Wells of England* (London, 1893), pp. 12, 87, 100, 109, 180, 185.

21. Fel and Hofer, *Proper Peasants*, p. 81; Edmund Schneeweis, *Serbokroatische Volkskunde* (Berlin, 1961), p. 5; Tokarev, *Religionznye Verovanie Vostochnoslavianakikh Narodov*, p. 52.

22. Abeghian, *Armenische Volksglaube*, p. 95.

23. Lisitsian, "Ocherki etnografii," p. 261.

24. Ibid., 260–61.

25. Bdoyan, *Hay Azgagrutyun*, pp. 187–88.

26. Abeghian, *Armenische Volksglaube*, p. 95; Lisitsian, "Ocherki etnografii," pp. 261–62; Bdoyan, *Hay Azgagrutyun*, pp. 188–89; Informant 47.

27. Avedis Aharonian, "The Ancient Beliefs of the Armenians according to Armenian Folklore" (Ph.D. diss., University of Lausanne, 1913), pp. 34–35. See also Bdoyan; *Hay Azgagrutyun*, pp. 189–90.

28. Lisitsian, "Ocherki etnografii," p. 262; Bdoyan, *Hay Azgagrutyun*, p. 191; Victor Turner, *The Ritual Process* (Chicago, 1969), chap. 5.

29. Lisitsian, "Ocherki etnografii," p. 263; Bdoyan, *Hay Azgagrutyun*, p. 193.

30. Ter Mowsesjanz, "Armenische Bauernhaus," p. 147, reports another observance that took place on the day before Easter, when the madagh was being prepared. Young villagers took a two-branch fork from a tree, peeled off the bark, and wove it into a shape resembling a modern tennis racquet. They dipped this into the blood of the sacrificial animal and placed it a field to ward off destructive influences, especially mice and grasshoppers. The Detroit informants did not verify this custom, however.

31. Melik-Pashayan, *Anahit*, p. 142; Lisitsian, "Ocherki etnografii," p. 263; Bdoyan, *Erkragordzakan*, p. 455.

32. Bdoyan, *Hay Azgagrutyun*, p. 194; Lisitsian, "Ocherki etnografii," p. 264.

33. Melik-Pashayan, *Anahit*, pp. 129–31, 147; Lisitsian, "Ocherki etnografii," p. 264.

34. Bdoyan, *Hay Azgagrutyun*, p. 195; A. A. Odabashyan, "Navasardyan tonokhmbutyunneri verapruknere," *Patma-banasirakan Handes* [Erevan], no. 3 (1974), pp. 113–26; V. H. Bdoyan, "Vanatur yev Amanor tsptyal pashtamunkneri hartsi shurje," *Lraber hasarakakan gitutyunneri*, no. 12 (1976), pp. 78–92. The celebration is mentioned in Shalian, trans., *David of Sassoun*, p. 204.

35. Benik E. Tumanian, "Measurement of Time in Ancient and Medieval Armenia," *Journal for the History of Astronomy* 5, pt. 2 (June 1974):95.

36. Lawson, *Modern Greek Folklore*, p. 303.

37. *Narody Kavkaza*, p. 141.

38. Jonas Balys, "Fastnachtsbrauche in Lituaen," *Schweizerisches Archiv für Volkskunde* 45–46 (1948–49):42; in *Healing Ritual* (London, 1935), p. 155, Patience Kemp reported that the Southern Slavs believed that swinging promoted health and hastened birth and marriage.

39. George A. Megas, *Greek Calendar Customs* (Athens, 1958), p. 76; Morgenstern, *Rites*, p. 157.

40. Lawson, *Modern Greek Folklore*, pp. 304–5.

41. Massé, *Persian Beliefs*, pp. 159–60.

42. Megas, *Greek Calendar Customs*, p. 147; B. A. Rybakov, "Kalendar IV v. iz zemli polian," *Sovetskaia Arkheologiia*, no. 4 (1962), p. 81.

43. Lawson, *Modern Greek Folklore*, p. 329; Massé, *Persian Beliefs*, pp. 266–269.

44. Massé, *Persian Beliefs*, p. 264; Kemp, *Healing Ritual*, p. 45.

45. Massé, *Persian Beliefs*, p. 304; and Snesarev, "Remnants of Pre-Islamic Beliefs," pp. 361–63.

46. Massé, *Persian Beliefs*, p. 97.

Chapter 7

1. The most helpful introductions to folk medicine in Europe and the Near East are L. I. Minko, "Magic Curing," pt. 1, *Soviet Anthropology and Archaeology* 12, no. 1 (Summer 1973):3–33; pt. 2, 12, no. 2 (Fall 1973):34–60; Iu. V. Bromlei and A. A. Voronov, "Folk Medicine as a Subject of Ethnographic Investigation," ibid. 18, no. 1 (Summer 1979):3–31. See also Richard Blum and Eva Blum, *Health and Healing in Rural Greece* (Stanford, Calif., 1965) and *Dangerous Hour;* Kemp, *Healing Ritual;* Phyllis Williams, *South Italian Folkways in Europe and America* (New Haven, Conn., 1938).

2. Lisitsian, "Ocherki etnografii," p. 258.

3. Clarence Maloney, ed., *The Evil Eye* (New York, 1976), pp. 8–10, 77–81, 240–55, 293–303; see also Blum and Blum, *Dangerous Hour*, p. 221; Irwin Sanders, *Balkan Village* (Lexington, Ky., 1949), p. 37.

4. Confirmed by Barrows, *On Horseback in Cappodocia*, p. 303.

5. The Southern Slavs also put a live coal in water; see Kemp, *Healing Ritual*, pp. 134–35; Olga Penavin, "Folk Medicine in a Settlement of the Szekely People in the Southern Banat Region of Yugoslavia," in *The Realm of the Extra Human: Ideas and Actions*, ed. Agehananda Bharati (The Hague, 1976), p. 422.

6. See also Maloney, ed., *Evil Eye*, pp. 8–10. Blunt, *People of Turkey*, 1:244, talks about various Christian preventatives for the evil eye, including sprinkling the person admired with holy water and fumigating him with the smoke from burning branches of the palms used on Palm Sunday. Ramsey, *Every-Day Life in Turkey*, pp. 60–64, describes a similar fumigation using the burning twig of an olive tree consecrated for the purpose by a priest. Barrows, *On Horseback in Cappodocia*, p. 302, reports that old skulls were hung in the fields to protect the grain from the evil eye, and that sometimes skulls were placed over the doors of houses. The Detroit informants did not confirm this latter custom.

7. There is some written literature on Armenian folk medicine, which the authors were unable to obtain: S. P. Zelinskii, *Materialy po Narodnoi Meditsine u Armian Nekotorykh Mestnostei Zakavkaz'ia* (Tbilisi, 1898): H. H. Sepetchyan, *Hayastanum Zhoghovrdi Mech Gortsatsvogh Gheghabujsere*, vol. 1 (Erevan, 1949); Garush Gasparyan, "Zhoghovrdakan bzhshkutyune hay panahyusutyan ev ditsabanutyan mech," *Lraber Hasarakakan Gitutyunneri*, no. 1 (1978), pp. 82–87. Ussher, *American Physician*, p. 13, writes that there was a 60 percent infant mortality rate before the second year. Smallpox was prevalent and often resulted in blindness.

8. Erwin H. Ackerknecht, "Primitive Surgery," *American Anthropologist* 49, no. 1 (1947):25–45.

9. M. Edith Durham, *High Albania* (London, 1909), p. 94; Kemp, *Healing Ritual*, p. 256.

10. Informant 16 reported that her family owned an ivory necklace. Every seven years, the beads divided, producing a necklace twice as long. If a family member suffered from scanty urine, a bead from this necklace was pulverized and given to him in water.

11. Lisitsian, "Ocherki etnografii," p. 259; Bdoyan, *Hay Azgagrutyun*, p. 171.

12. Lisitsian, "Ocherki etnografii," p. 258; Bdoyan, *Hay Azgagrutyun*, p. 171.

13. Lisitsian, "Ocherki etnografii," pp. 258, 260; Massé, *Persian Beliefs*, p. 90.

14. Lisitsian, "Ocherki etnografii," p. 33; Massé, *Persian Beliefs*, p. 98.

15. See Ramsey, *Every-Day Life in Turkey*, pp. 90–98; Van Lennep, *Travels*, 1:287–88; Barrows, *On Horseback in Cappodocia*, pp. 77–79, for descriptions of Armenian cemeteries and some of the prohibitions placed on them.

16. Mircea Eliade, *Shamanism* (New York, 1964), pp. 202, 395–96n; Grigolia, *Custom and Justice*, p. 44; Felix J. Oinas, "Russian 'Golubec' Grave Markers, Etc., and Some Notions of the Soul," *International Journal of Slavic Linguistics and Poetics* 8 (1964):77–86; Stith Thompson, *Motif Index of Folk Literature* (Bloomington, Ind., 1956), p. 503; Robert Hertz, *Death and the Right Hand* (Glencoe, Ill., 1960), p. 48; R. B. Onians, *The Origins of European Thought* (Cambridge, 1951), pp. 254, 289; Schneewies, *Serbokroatische Volkskunde*, p. 107; Massé, p. 225.

17. Eliade, *Shamanism*, p. 207.

18. Kurt Ranke, *Indogermanische Totenverehrung: Der Dreissignste und Vierzigste Tag im Totenkult der Indogermaner* (Helsinki, 1951); Massé, *Persian Beliefs*, pp. 94, 99; Lawson, *Modern Greek Folklore*, pp. 486–87.

19. Mary K. Matossian, "Birds, Bees, and Barley: Pagan Origins of Armenian Spring Rituals," *Armenian Review* 32, no. 3 (Sept. 1979):292–302; V. Ia. Propp, *Russkie Agrarnye Prazdniki* (Leningrad, 1963), pp. 20–21; Morgenstern, *Rites*, pp. 154–60; F. K. Litsas, "Rousalia: The Ritual Worship of the Dead," in Bharati, ed., *Realm of the Extra Human*, pp. 447–65.

20. Clara C. Rice, *Persian Women and Their Ways* (London, 1923), p. 264; Grigolia, *Custom and Justice*, p. 50.

SELECTED BIBLIOGRAPHY

Abbot, John. *The Keys to Power.* London, 1932.

Abeghian, Manuk. *Der Armenische Volksglaube.* Leipzig, 1899.

Afanas'ev, A. N. *Poeticheskie vosrenie slavian na prirodu.* Moscow, 1865–69.

Aharonian, Avedis. *The Ancient Beliefs of the Armenians according to Armenian Folklore.* Lausanne, 1913.

Aharonian, G. *Husseynik.* Boston, 1966.

Ainsworth, W. F. *Travels and Researches in Asia Minor, Mesopotamia, Chaldea, and Armenia.* 2 vols. London, 1842.

Ananikian, Mardiros. "Armenian Mythology." In *Mythology of All Races,* edited by John MacCulloch. Boston, 1925.

Anderson, Rufus. *History of the Missions of the American Board of Commissioners for Foreign Missions to the Oriental Churches.* 2 vols. Boston, 1873.

"Armiane." In *Narody Kavkaza,* vol. 2, pp. 435–601. Moscow, 1962.

Atamian, Sarkis. *The Armenian Community.* New York, 1955.

————. "The Traditional Armenian Family in Turkish Armenia." *Hairenik Weekly,* 13 Oct.–24 Nov. 1949.

Atikian, Martha B., and Atikian, Hagop. *Armenian Names.* N.p., 1973.

Barton, James. *Daybreak in Turkey.* Boston, 1908.

Barrows, J. O. *On Horseback in Cappodocia.* Boston, 1884.

Bdoyan, V. H. *Erkragordzakan mshakuyte Hayastanum* [Agriculture in Armenia]. Erevan. 1972.

————. *Hay Azgagrutyun: Hamarot Urvagits* [Armenian ethnography: brief outline]. Erevan, 1974.

Blum, Richard, and Blum, Eva. *Health and Healing in Rural Greece.* Stanford, Calif., 1965.

————. *The Dangerous Hour.* New York, 1970.

Blunt, Mrs. John Elyah. *The People of Turkey.* 2 vols. London, 1878.

Brice, William C., ed. *The Environmental History of the Near and Middle East.* New York, 1978.

Bryce, James B. *Transcaucasia and Ararat.* 4th ed. London, 1896.

Buxton, N., and Buxton H. *Travels and Politics in Armenia.* New York, 1914.

Campbell, John K. *Honour, Family, and Patronage.* Oxford, 1964.

Crawford, O. G. S. *The Eye Goddess.* New York, n. d.

Creagh, James. *Armenians, Koords, and Turks.* 2 vols. London, 1880.

Davey, Richard. *The Sultan and His Subjects.* London, 1907.

Davis, E. J. *Life in Asiatic Turkey.* London, 1879.

Davis, John. *People of the Mediterranean.* London, 1977.

Dekorativnoe Iskusstvo Srednevekovoi Armenii. Leningrad, 1971.

Denton, W. *The Christians in Turkey.* London, 1863.

Der Nersessian, Sirarpie. *The Armenians.* New York, 1970.

Durham, Mary Edith. *High Albania.* London, 1909.

————. *Some Tribal Origins, Laws, and Customs of the Balkans.* London, 1928.

Eliade, Mircea. *Patterns in Comparative Religion.* New York, 1964.

Essabel, Paul. "The Door and Threshold in Armenian Folklore." *Western Folklore* 20 (1961):265–73.

Fel, Edit, and Hofer, Tamas. *Proper Peasants: Traditional Life in a Hungarian Village.* Chicago, 1969.

Garnett, Lucy. *Home Life in Turkey.* New York, 1909.

————. *The Women of Turkey and Their Folklore.* 2 vols. London, 1890–91.

Greene, Frederik Davis. *The Rule of the Turk.* New York, 1896.

Greene, Joseph K. *Leavening the Levant.* Boston, 1916.

Grigolia, Alexander. *Custom and Justice in the Caucasus: The Georgian Highlanders.* Philadelphia, Pa., 1939.

Gulick, John. *The Middle East: An Anthropological Perspective.* Pacific Palisades, Calif., 1976.

Halpern, Joel M. *A Serbian Village.* New York, 1958.

Hamlin, Cyrus. *Among the Turks.* New York, 1878.

Harris, James Rendell, and Harris, Helen B. *Letters from Armenia.* New York, 1897.

Haxthausen, August von. *Transcaucasia.* London, 1854.

Heers, Jacques. *Family Clans in the Middle Ages.* New York, 1977.

Hepworth, George H. *On Horseback through Armenia.* New York, 1898.

Hodgetts, E. A. Brayley. *Round about Armenia.* London, 1896.

Hoogasian-Villa, Susie, ed. *One Hundred Armenian Tales and Their Folkloristic Relevance.* Detroit, Mich., 1966.

Karapetian, E. T. *Rodstvennaia Gruppa 'Azg' u Armian* [The 'azg' kin group among the Armenians]. Erevan, 1966.

————. *Armianskaia Semeinaia Obshchina* [The Armenian extended family household]. Erevan, 1958.

Karpat, Kemal H., ed. *The Ottoman State and Its Place in World History.* London, 1974.

Kemp, Patience. *Healing Ritual: Studies in the Technique and Tradition of the Eastern Slavs.* London, 1935.

Lang, David M. *Armenia, Cradle of Civilization.* London, 1978.

Lawson, John C. *Modern Greek Folklore and Ancient Greek Religion.* New Hyde Park, New York, 1964.

Lisitsian, S. D. "Ocherki etnografii dorevoliutsionnoi Armenii" [Outline of the ethnography of prerevolutionary Armenia]. In *Kavkazskii Etnograficheskii* Sbornik, vol. 1 (Moscow, 1955), pp. 182–272.

Lynch, H. F. B. *Armenia, Travels and Studies.* 2 vols. London, 1900–1901.

MacDonald, Alex. *The Land of Ararat; or, Up the Roof of the World*. London, 1895.

Magnarella, Paul J. *The Peasant Venture: Tradition, Migration, and Change among Georgian Peasants in Turkey*. Boston, 1979.

————, and Turkdogan, Orhan. "Descent, Affinity, and Ritual Relations in Eastern Turkey." *American Anthropologist* 75, no. 5 (1973):1626–33.

Maloney, Clarence, ed. *The Evil Eye*. New York, 1976.

Manandyan, Hakob. *The Trade and Cities of Armenia in Relation to Ancient World Trade*. Lisbon, 1965.

Massé, Henri. *Persian Beliefs and Customs*. New Haven, Conn., 1954.

Matossian, Mary. "Birds, Bees, and Barley: Pagan Origins of Armenian Spring Rituals." *Armenian Review* 32, no. 3 (Sept. 1979):292–302.

Morgenstern, Julian. *Rites of Birth, Marriage, Death, and Kindred Occasions among the Semites*. New York, 1973.

Morier, James. *Journey through Pesia, Armenia, and Asia Minor to Constantinople in the Year 1808–09*. Philadelphia. Pa., 1816.

Odabashyan, A. A. "Navasardyan tonokhmbutyunneri verapruknere." *Patma-banasirakan Handes*, no. 3 (1974):113–26.

Paine, Caroline. *Tent and Harem*. New York, 1859.

Parmelee, Moses P. *Life Scenes around the Mountains of Ararat*. Boston, 1868.

Parsatanyan, R. S. *Hayastani Aroghdjapahutyan Patmutyun*. Erevan, 1973.

Peristiany, J. G., ed. *Mediterranean Family Structure*. Cambridge, 1976.

Pierce, Joe E. *Life in a Turkish Village*. New York, 1964.

Prime, E. D. G. *Forty Years in the Turkish Empire; or, the Memories of Reverend William Goodell*. New York, 1876.

Ramsey, Mrs. W. M. *Every-Day Life in Turkey*. London, 1897.

Rice, Clara Colliver. *Persian Women and Their Ways*. London, 1923.

Richter, Julius. *A History of the Protestant Missions in the Near East*. London, 1910.

Sarkisian, E. K. *Politika Osmanskogo Pravitel'stva v Zapadnoi Armenii i Derzhavy v Poslednem Chetverti XXIX i Nachale XX vv*. Erevan, 1972.

Schneider, Mrs. E. C. A. *Letters from Broosa, Asia Minor*. Chambersburg, Pa., 1846.

Sertel, A. K. "Ritual Kinship in Eastern Turkey." *Anthropological Quarterly* 44, no. 1 (1971):35–50.

Shaw, Stanford J., and Shaw, Ezel Kural. *History of the Ottoman Empire and Turkey*. New York, 1976–77.

Smith, Catherine D. *Western Mediterranean Europe*. London, 1977.

Stirling, Paul. *Turkish Village*. New York, 1965.

Tavernier, Jean-Baptiste. *Collections of Travels through Turkey into Persia and the East Indies*. London, 1684.

Tcheraz, Minas. *L'Orient inédit*. Paris, 1912.

Ter Mowsesjanz, Parsadan. "Der Armenische Bauernhaus." *Anthropologische Gesellschaft in Wien* 22 (1892):125–72.

Tokarev, S. A. *Religioznye Verovanie Vostochnoslavianskikh Narodov xix-Nachala xx v*. Moscow, 1957.

Tozer, Henry F. *Turkish Armenia and Eastern Asia Minor*. London, 1881.

Ussher, Clarence E., and Knapp, Grace H. *An American Physician in Turkey*. Boston, 1917.

Van Lennep, Henry. *Bible Lands: Their Modern Customs and Manners.* New York, 1875.

————. *Travels in Little Known Parts of Asia Minor.* 2 vols. London, 1870.

Wallis, Wilson D. "Some Phases of Armenian Social Life." *American Anthropologist* 25 (1923):582–84.

Wheeler, Mrs. Crosby H. *Missions in Eden.* New York, 1899.

Yernchakyan, Nvard. "Lusine Hay Zhoghoordakan havataliknerum ev sovorwitnerum." *Lraber Hasarakadan Gitutyunneri,* no. 6 (1979):53–60.

Zelenin, D. K. "Magicheskaia funktsiia primitivnykh orudii." *Izvestiia Akademii Nauk, Otdelenie Obshchestvennykh Nauk,* no. 6 (1931).

Zelinskii, S. P. *Materialy po Narodnoe Meditsine u Armian Nekotorykh Mestnostei Zakavkaz'ia.* Tbilisi, 1898.

Zouche, Robert N. C. G. C. *Armenia: A Year at Erzeroom.* London, 1854.

INDEX

Susie (Soseh) Hoogasian Villa grew up in a predominantly Armenian section of Detroit and received her early education at the Zavarian Armenian School. She earned a B.S. in education (1944) and an M.A. in English (1948) from Wayne State University, and studied under Stith Thompson at the Indiana University Folklore Institute. She was a member of the Department of English, Oakland Community College. Mrs. Villa's scholarly career was devoted to capturing and preserving traditional Armenian culture. Her *One Hundred Armenian Tales and Their Folkloristic Relevance* (Wayne State University Press, 1966) tied for first place in the University of Chicago Folklore Prize competition.

Mary Kilbourne Matossian was educated at Stanford University (B.A., 1951; Ph.D., 1955) and the American University of Beirut (M.A., 1952). She has been a research fellow at the Center for Middle Eastern Studies and a research associate at the Russian Research Center, both at Harvard University, and had taught at the State University of New York at Buffalo. She is currently associate professor of history at the University of Maryland. Dr. Matossian is the author of several articles and of *The Impact of Soviet Policies in Armenia* (1962).

The manuscript was edited by Sherwyn T. Carr, Alice Nigoghosian, and Doreen Broder. The book was designed by Mary Primeau. The map was drawn by Elizabeth Hanson and Patrick Callahan.

The typeface for the text is Times Roman, based on a design by Stanley Morison about 1932. The display face is Times Roman.

The book is printed on 60 lb. Glatfelter B-31 textpaper. The book is bound in Holliston Mills' Natural finish cloth over binder's boards.

Manufactured in the United States of America.